Getting Started

with Windows® 10 and Microsoft® Edge

plus OneDrive™ and OneNote®

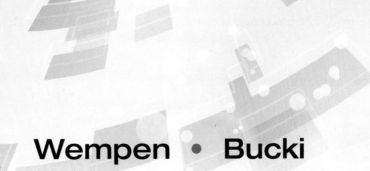

Wempen • Bucki

PARADIGM
EDUCATION SOLUTIONS

St. Paul

Director of Editorial: Christine Hurney
Senior Editor: Cheryl Drivdahl
Reviewers: Jan Marrelli, Audrey Roggenkamp, Ian Rutkosky, Nita Rutkosky, and Denise Seguin
Testers: Jeff Johnson and Rob Neilly
Director of Production: Timothy W. Larson
Senior Production Editor: Lori Michelle Ryan
Cover Designer: Sara Schmidt Boldon
Text Designer: Valerie King
Senior Design and Production Specialists: Valerie King and Jack Ross
Copy Editor: Sarah Kearin
Supplement Copy Editors: Joanna Chloe Grote, Traci Post, and Penny Stuart
Proofreader: Nikki Kallio
Indexer: Ina Gravitz
VP and Director of Digital Projects: Chuck Bratton
Digital Projects Manager: Tom Modl
Digital Learning Manager: Troy Weets
Director of Marketing: Lara Weber McLellan
Web Developer: Blue Earth Interactive
Video Producer: Braahmam, Hurix Systems

Care has been taken to verify the accuracy of information presented in this book. However, the authors, editors, and publisher cannot accept responsibility for web, email, newsgroup, or chat room subject matter or content, or for consequences from the application of the information in this book, and make no warranty, expressed or implied, with respect to its content.

Trademarks: Microsoft is a trademark or registered trademark of Microsoft Corporation in the United States and/or other countries. Some of the product names and company names included in this book have been used for identification purposes only and may be trademarks or registered trade names of their respective manufacturers and sellers. The authors, editors, and publisher disclaim any affiliation, association, or connection with, or sponsorship or endorsement by, such owners.

Photo Credits: Cover blinkblink/Shutterstock.com; **xi** ©Oleksiy Mark/Shutterstock.com; **x** © sambrogio/istock (left); courtesy of Sandisk corporation (center); © gmnicholas/istock; **41** Google and the Google logo are registered trademarks of Google Inc., used with permission; **42** Google and the Google logo are registered trademarks of Google Inc., used with permission; all screen captures of Microsoft products are used with permission from Microsoft.

We have made every effort to trace the ownership of all copyrighted material and to secure permission from copyright holders. In the event of any question arising as to the use of any material, we will be pleased to make the necessary corrections in future printings.

Paradigm Publishing, Inc., is independent from Microsoft Corporation and not affiliated with Microsoft in any manner.

ISBN 978-0-76386-662-4 (print)
ISBN 978-0-76386-663-1 (digital)

© 2016 by Paradigm Publishing, Inc.
875 Montreal Way
St. Paul, MN 55102
Email: educate@emcp.com
Website: ParadigmCollege.com

Printed in the United States of America

24 23 22 21 20 19 18   4 5 6 7 8 9 10

Contents

Workbook: Chapter Review and Assessment

Note: Workbook pages are available in the ebook.

Preface

Getting Started with Windows® 10 and Microsoft® Edge uses a simple, visual approach to teach the necessary skills for using the Windows 10 operating system and Microsoft Edge web browser, plus OneDrive and OneNote. It also introduces the Office Online apps, tools for creating screenshots, and the Snipping Tool. This brief program will help you gain the proficiency needed to open and use applications, navigate between and within applications, manage files, get information from the Internet, and share files and information on a PC with Windows 10 installed. In addition, it will help you master basic skills for customizing and maintaining the Windows operating system.

Chapter Features

The following guide shows how this textbook and its digital resources uses a visual, step-by-step, competency-based approach to teach the basic skills you need to use a PC running Windows 10 successfully at home, school, or work.

SNAP Resources

SNAP icons in the margins of the textbook are accompanied by blue text listing exercises and assessments that are available in SNAP. If you are a SNAP user, go to your SNAP Assignments page to complete the activities.

Interactive Student Resources

Orange icons in the margins of the textbook indicate interactive resources that are available through the links menu in your ebook.

Precheck quizzes test your knowledge of the chapter content before you study the material. Use the results to help focus your study on the skills you need to learn.

Tutorials guide you through the steps for the skills and then allow you to practice on your own. These interactive tutorials include simple instructions and optional help.

Student data files are needed to complete some of the skills and assessments in this book. You will learn how to download these files to a USB flash drive in Chapter 2, and then upload them to your OneDrive account in Chapter 4.

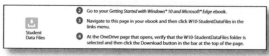

Online Extras expand on the topics covered in the textbook. Read these brief summaries to discover additional features and functionality.

Recheck quizzes at the end of each chapter enable you to recheck your understanding of the chapter content. You may recheck your understanding at any time and as many times as you wish.

A **Workbook** , included in the ebook, provides study tools (including PowerPoint presentations and Tips & Hints), exercises, and assessments to help you review the features and skills covered in each chapter.

Textbook Elements

Clear and concise text and screen captures teach essential concepts, features, and skills in an easy-to-understand format.

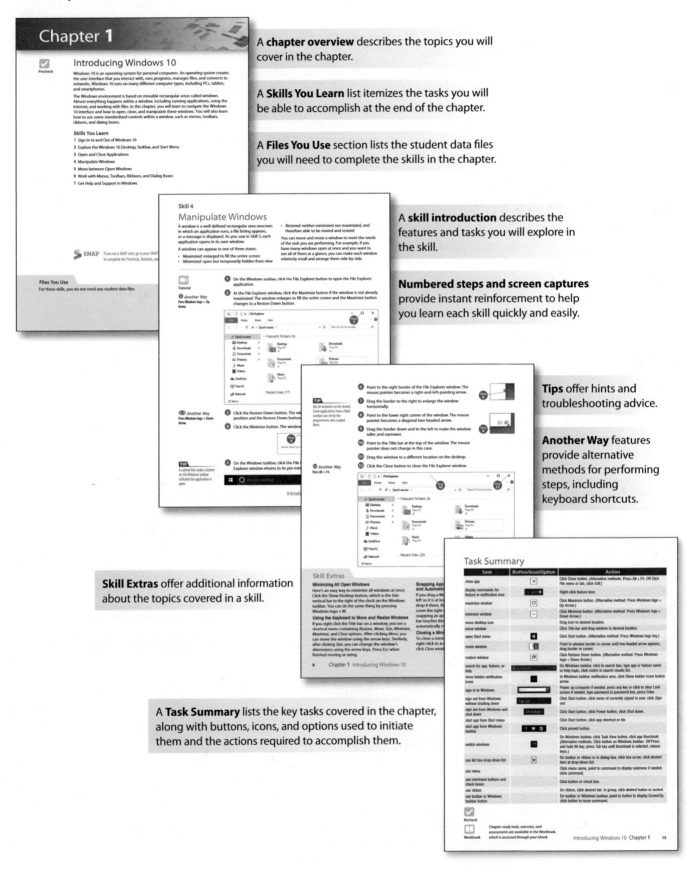

A **chapter overview** describes the topics you will cover in the chapter.

A **Skills You Learn** list itemizes the tasks you will be able to accomplish at the end of the chapter.

A **Files You Use** section lists the student data files you will need to complete the skills in the chapter.

A **skill introduction** describes the features and tasks you will explore in the skill.

Numbered steps and screen captures provide instant reinforcement to help you learn each skill quickly and easily.

Tips offer hints and troubleshooting advice.

Another Way features provide alternative methods for performing steps, including keyboard shortcuts.

Skill Extras offer additional information about the topics covered in a skill.

A **Task Summary** lists the key tasks covered in the chapter, along with buttons, icons, and options used to initiate them and the actions required to accomplish them.

Workbook Review and Assessment

You will access the Workbook through your ebook. The Workbook provides a variety of materials you can use to check your understanding of the concepts and features covered in the textbook. Complete the Workbook activities to demonstrate your ability to apply the skills taught. For each chapter, you will find the following items:

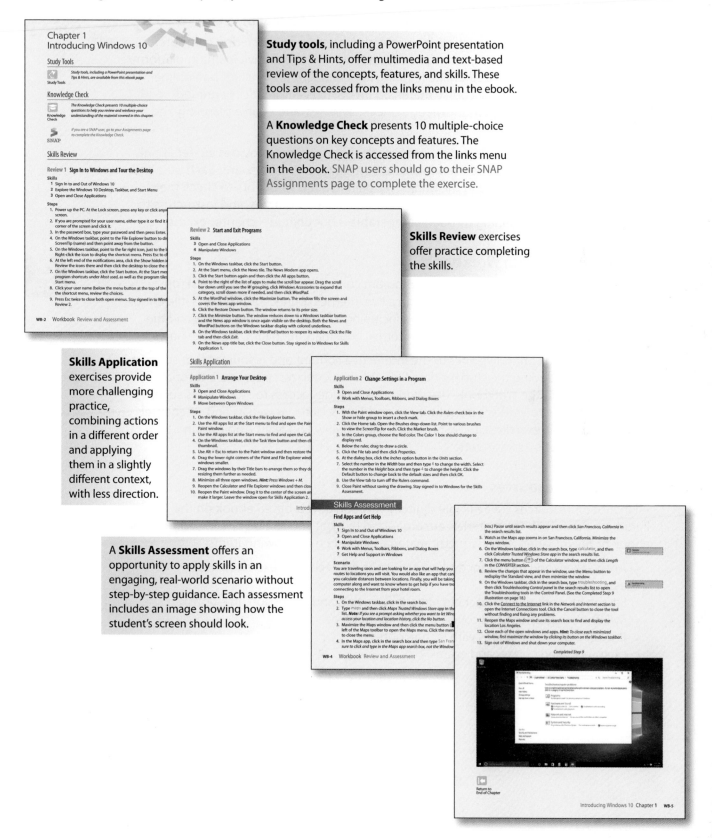

Study tools, including a PowerPoint presentation and Tips & Hints, offer multimedia and text-based review of the concepts, features, and skills. These tools are accessed from the links menu in the ebook.

A **Knowledge Check** presents 10 multiple-choice questions on key concepts and features. The Knowledge Check is accessed from the links menu in the ebook. SNAP users should go to their SNAP Assignments page to complete the exercise.

Skills Review exercises offer practice completing the skills.

Skills Application exercises provide more challenging practice, combining actions in a different order and applying them in a slightly different context, with less direction.

A **Skills Assessment** offers an opportunity to apply skills in an engaging, real-world scenario without step-by-step guidance. Each assessment includes an image showing how the student's screen should look.

Course Components

The *Getting Started with Windows® 10 and Microsoft® Edge* textbook contains the essential content students will need to master the key concepts and skills covered. Additional resources are provided by the following digital components.

SNAP Web-Based Training and Assessment for Microsoft® Office 2016

SNAP is a web-based program offering an interactive venue for mastering computer skills. SNAP includes a learning management system with an adaptive learning platform to create a more individualized online learning experience. It also includes an online grade book; easy access to all course materials; interactive, automatically graded versions of the end-of-chapter Knowledge Check exercises; and course planning and delivery tools.

The SNAP course offers a quiz and exam for each chapter. It also provides an item bank for each chapter, which can be used to create custom quizzes and exams. Each quiz and exam item is aligned to a skill in the book. This pairing allows students to check their understanding and track their progress through the chapter quizzes, and instructors to assess student understanding through comparable—but unique—chapter exams.

Student eBook with Workbook

The student ebook provides access to all program content from any device (desktop, tablet, and smartphone) anywhere, through a live Internet connection. The versatile ebook platform features dynamic navigation tools including a linked table of contents and the ability to jump to specific pages, search for terms, bookmark, highlight, and take notes.

The student ebook offers live links to the interactive content and resources that support the textbook, including the student data files; Precheck quizzes; interactive tutorials; Online Extras; and the Workbook. The Workbook includes access to study tools such as chapter-based PowerPoint presentations and Tips & Hints, as well as end-of-chapter Knowledge Check exercises. It also provides Skills Review and Skills Application exercises, and Skills Assessments.

Instructor eResources

All instructor resources are available digitally through a web-based ebook on the Paradigm Bookshelf. The materials are organized by type and can be previewed from the ebook or downloaded. The instructor materials include the following items:

- Answer keys and rubrics for evaluating responses to chapter exercises and assessments
- Lesson blueprints with teaching hints, lecture tips, and discussion questions
- Syllabus suggestions and course planning resources
- PowerPoint presentations with lecture notes
- Chapter-based quizzes and exams

Getting Started

Microsoft Windows 10 is the latest version of Windows, the most popular operating system in the world for personal computers. This book teaches you how to use Windows 10 to accomplish basic tasks on a personal computer, such as running programs and managing files, as well as how to customize and maintain the Windows operating system. It also introduces the Microsoft Edge browser and shows you how to find information on the Internet.

In addition, this book covers Microsoft applications designed to optimize your use of a Windows 10 computer in a personal, work, or academic environment. You will learn how to access OneDrive, a secure online storage location, and how to use Office Online apps. You will also learn how to take screenshots and how to collect, organize, and share research data using OneNote.

Your Textbook and Student Resources

This book comes in two versions: an ebook, and an ebook plus a printed textbook. The ebook provides access to the Precheck and Recheck quizzes, student data files, interactive tutorials, Online Extras, end-of-chapter workbook materials (including PowerPoint presentations, review exercises, and assessments), and other student resources that support the text. To complete a course based on this book, you will need the ebook plus a computer that has an Internet connection and the Windows 10 operating system with the Microsoft Edge browser.

The student data files you will need to complete some of the skills, exercises, and assessments in the textbook and workbook are accessed from the ebook. Chapter 2 teaches you how to download the student data files from the ebook to a USB flash drive, and Chapter 4 teaches you how to upload the student data files from the USB flash drive to your OneDrive account. You do not need any student data files for Chapter 1.

Hardware and Software Requirements

Your book is designed for a computer running a standard installation of Microsoft Windows 10 Home or Microsoft Windows 10 Pro on a desktop or notebook PC. To run this operating system, your computer should have the following capabilities:

- Processor: 1 gigahertz (GHz) or faster
- RAM: Minimum 1 gigabyte (GB) for the 32-bit version or 2 GB for the 64-bit version
- Free hard disk space: 16 GB
- Graphics card: Microsoft DirectX 9 graphics device with WDDM driver
- Monitor/screen: Screen captures in this book were created using a screen resolution display of 1366 x 768. If you would like your screen to match the images in the book, see Chapter 6, Skill 3, pages 83–84 for instructions on changing the resolution of your monitor.

Certain chapters and skills in this book also assume that you have the following additional features:

- Internet access (for downloading the student data files, sending email, and using online apps)
- A USB flash drive (for storing student data files)
- A printer
- **Optional:** Speakers or headphones, and a microphone (for communicating with Cortana)

Note that Windows 10 will update over time. For that reason you may see discrepancies between the screen captures in this textbook and the interface on your computer screen.

Starting Up and Shutting Down

If you are using a computer in a school lab environment, you might not need to start it up or shut it down, because many labs leave their computers on throughout the day, turning them off only at night. If you are using your own computer, though, you will want to know how to turn it on and off.

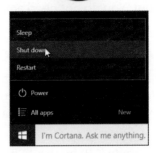

- **To turn on the computer:** On the computer, press the power button, which loads the Windows 10 operating system. A sign-in prompt appears when Windows has finished loading. To sign in, see Chapter 1, Skill 1.
- **To turn off the computer:** On the Windows taskbar, click the Start button, click Power, and then click the *Shut Down* option. Shutting down in this way also signs you out. To sign out without shutting down, see Chapter 1, Skill 1.

Creating an Account on a Windows PC

In a school or work setting, you will probably be assigned a user name and password to use when signing in to Windows 10. The user name may be an email address. If you already have a user name and password, there is no need to create another one to use with this book.

If you do not already have a user name and password, you will need to create a new user account. To do this, you must first be signed in to Windows 10 using an account with Administrator privileges and connected to the Internet. You must also either have an existing email address or be prepared to create one during the process. Ask your instructor for help if needed. After you have signed in to the computer using the Administrator account, complete the following steps:

1. On the Windows taskbar, click the Start button and then click *Settings*.

2. In the Settings app, click Accounts.

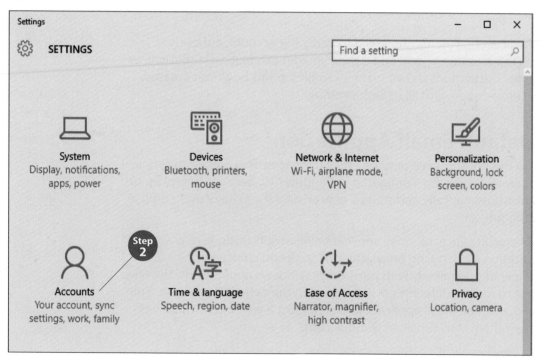

3. In the Navigation pane of the Accounts section, click *Family & other users* (or *Other users* on some systems).

4. In the right pane, click *Add someone else to this PC*.

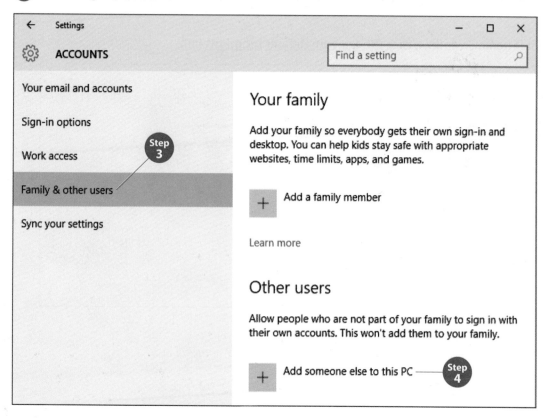

5 Follow the prompts that appear, filling in information as requested, to create the account. The prompts you see depend on whether you are creating a new email address or using an existing one, and whether the email address you are using has previously been registered with Microsoft.

After you create the account, you may be asked to verify the account, either by responding to an email message or entering a code you get in a text message. Follow the prompts to do so. The account shown in the examples in this book was created using the Express Setup option with all default settings.

Setting a Default Email Application

A few of the skills in this book involve sending email messages. This process is simple if you have a default email application configured in Windows 10, because Windows 10 opens the application automatically and starts a new email. All you have to do is fill in the recipient and the subject.

When you install Microsoft Office, its email application Microsoft Outlook may set itself as the default application for handling email. Outlook is a good choice for the skills in this book because it works seamlessly with most other Windows applications. However, you can also choose to make a different email application the default if you wish. Your choice of application must be a real application, and not just a web interface for web-based email such as Yahoo! Mail, Gmail, or Outlook.com.

To set your default email application, follow these steps:

1 On the Windows taskbar, type default in the search box.

2 In the search results list, click *Default Programs Desktop app.* If there are two by that same name, as shown here, choose the one with the green circle containing a check mark.

3 In the Default Programs window, click the Set your default programs link.

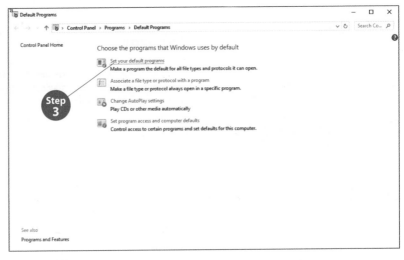

4 In the *Programs* list box of the Set Default Programs app, click the desired email program, such as *Outlook 2016*. **Note:** *You may need to scroll to locate the desired program.*

5 In the right pane, click *Set this program as default*.

6 Click the OK button to close the Set Default Programs window.

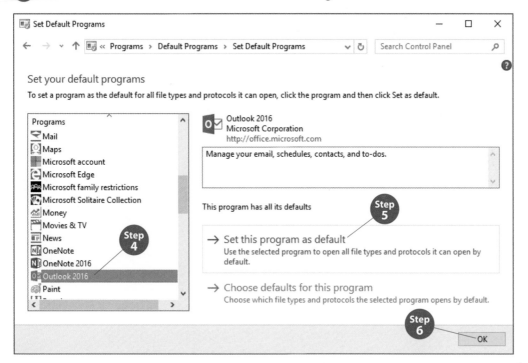

7 Click the Close button to close the Default Programs window.

Using a Touchscreen

This book assumes you are working on a desktop or notebook PC, and instructions refer to the keyboard and mouse as the primary input devices. However, if you have a touchscreen, you may use it for input in most cases. Note that touchscreens are different from other types of input devices, and you will need some special skills to use this form of device. Here are a few important terms you should know:

 Tap (or touch). Tap the screen with one finger, pressing and quickly releasing on the same spot. You tap to make a selection or issue a command.

 **Stretch (or unpinch).** Touch two fingers to the screen in adjacent spots and then drag the fingers farther apart. You stretch to zoom in (and display a smaller area).

 Rotate. Touch two fingers on the desired object or area and then drag them in a circular motion.

 Pinch. Touch two fingers to the screen in different spots and then drag the fingers together. You pinch to zoom out (and display a larger area).

 Drag (or slide or swipe). Touch one finger to the screen and then slide it along the surface. You drag to perform a variety of functions, depending on the software and context. For example, dragging can open menu bars, exit applications, scroll the display, or move items around on the screen.

Chapter 1

Precheck

Introducing Windows 10

Windows 10 is an operating system for personal computers. An *operating system* creates the user interface that you interact with, runs programs, manages files, and connects to networks. Windows 10 runs on many different computer types, including PCs, tablets, and smartphones.

The Windows environment is based on movable rectangular areas called *windows*. Almost everything happens within a window, including running applications, using the Internet, and working with files. In this chapter, you will learn to navigate the Windows 10 interface and how to open, close, and manipulate these windows. You will also learn how to use some standardized controls within a window, such as menus, toolbars, ribbons, and dialog boxes.

Skills You Learn

1 Sign In to and Out of Windows 10

2 Explore the Windows 10 Desktop, Taskbar, and Start Menu

3 Open and Close Applications

4 Manipulate Windows

5 Move between Open Windows

6 Work with Menus, Toolbars, Ribbons, and Dialog Boxes

7 Get Help and Support in Windows

 **SNAP** If you are a SNAP user, go to your SNAP Assignments page to complete the Precheck, Tutorials, and Recheck.

Files You Use

For these skills, you do not need any student data files.

Sign In to and Out of Windows 10

To use Windows, you must *sign in*. Signing in usually involves selecting a user account and then typing a password. Depending on how your school's PCs are configured, you may already have been assigned a user name and password with which to sign in to Windows PCs. If so, use them in the following steps. If not, ask your instructor what user name and password to use.

When you finish your Windows session, you should *sign out*. Signing out shuts down any running applications and data files and disconnects from any user-specific resources, such as your personal folders. If nobody will be using the computer for a while, you can also *shut down* as you sign out. Shutting down exits Windows entirely and turns off the computer's power.

Tutorial

TIP

The Lock screen appears when nobody is signed in to Windows or when the signed-in user has locked the PC.

TIP

In Step 4, if you are not prompted for your user name and do not see it in the lower left corner of the screen, click *Other user* to display the prompt.

7–9 *Another Way*

Right-click the Start button, point to *Shut down or sign out*, and then click *Sign out*.

Online Extras

1. Power up the PC, if it is not already on.

2. If you see the Windows desktop, someone is already signed in to the PC and you need to sign out (see Steps 7–9).

3. If you see the Lock screen (displaying a full-screen graphic with the time and date), press any key or click anywhere on the screen to open the Sign-in screen.

4. If you are prompted for your user name, type it.

5. In the password box, type the password for your account.

6. Press Enter to display the desktop.

7. Click the Start button.

8. At the Start menu, click your user name.

9. At the menu, click *Sign out* to sign out of Windows without shutting down your computer.

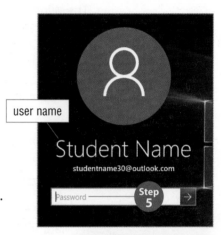

Skill Extra

Signing Out of Windows and Shutting Down

Sometimes you might want to turn off the computer completely, not just sign out. To do so, click the Start button, click *Power* at the Start menu, and then click *Shut down*. Alternatively, click *Sleep* to place the computer in a low-power state without shutting it down.

Skill 2

Explore the Windows 10 Desktop, Taskbar, and Start Menu

In this skill you will learn about the basic components of the Windows 10 interface: the desktop, the taskbar, and the Start menu.

Desktop

The *desktop* is the main Windows screen that you see after you sign in. As you open windows, the windows appear on top of the desktop.

An *icon* is a small picture representing a file, folder, or program. By default there is one icon on the desktop: Recycle Bin (covered in Chapter 2). However, you may see others on your desktop. Some icons are shortcuts. A *shortcut* is a pointer to a file or folder located elsewhere. For example, when some applications install, they create shortcuts on the desktop so you can run them more easily.

Windows Taskbar

The *Windows taskbar* is the bar across the bottom of the desktop. At the far left end is the *Start button*. Clicking the Start button opens the *Start menu*, which is a gateway to running installed applications and accessing system settings and utilities.

To the right of the Start button is a *search box*, which provides access to Cortana, the Windows 10 help and search feature. Cortana is covered in Chapter 3. The prompt that appears in your search box may be different from what's shown here.

The Windows taskbar can hold pinned buttons for easy access to commonly used applications. A *pinned button* is a shortcut that stays where it is pinned. The default pinned shortcuts on the Windows taskbar include Task View, Microsoft Edge (covered in Chapter 3), File Explorer (covered in Chapter 2), and Store. You can also pin your own favorite applications there (see the Online Extras at the end of this skill).

The Windows taskbar also displays a button for each open window. You can switch to an open window by clicking its button there. A button for an open window looks very much like a pinned shortcut, except that it has a colored line under it.

At the right end of the Windows taskbar is the *notification area*. It contains buttons that represent programs and utilities that are running in the background. You can right-click any of these buttons to see a menu for managing it. At the far right end of the Windows taskbar is a clock.

Start Menu

Clicking the Start button opens the Start menu. The Start menu contains shortcuts to many commonly used applications and utilities. Some of the shortcuts on the Start menu appear as *tiles* (colored rectangles). The main function of the Start menu is to open applications, which is covered in Skill 4.

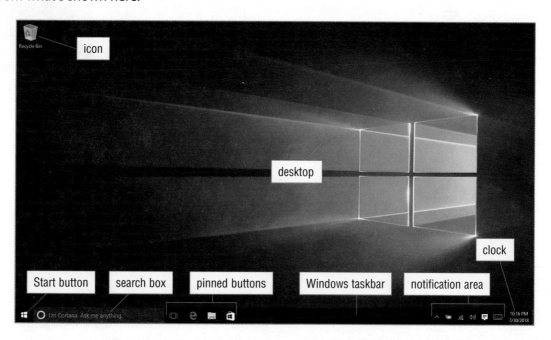

1 Sign in to Windows if needed, to display the desktop.

2 Drag the Recycle Bin icon to the upper right corner of the desktop.

3 Drag the Recycle Bin icon back to its original location.

4 Point to the yellow folder button pinned to the Windows taskbar and read the ScreenTip that displays its name: *File Explorer*.

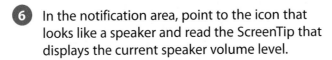

5 Repeat Step 4 to see the names of all the other pinned buttons on the Windows taskbar.

6 In the notification area, point to the icon that looks like a speaker and read the ScreenTip that displays the current speaker volume level.

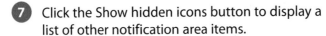

7 Click the Show hidden icons button to display a list of other notification area items.

8 Click away from the list to close it without making a selection.

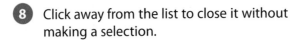

9 Right-click the speaker icon to display a shortcut menu of speaker options.

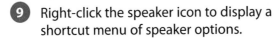

10 Click away from the menu to close it without making a selection.

11 Click the Start button.

12 Click *Settings*.

13 At the Settings window, notice the different options for customizing Windows. Click the Close button to close the window without changing any settings.

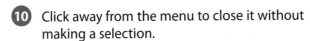

Skill Extra

Dragging

To drag an icon with the mouse, position the mouse pointer over the item and then hold down the left mouse button as you move the mouse. To drag on a touchscreen, touch the item and then move your finger across the surface of the touchscreen.

Skill 3
Open and Close Applications

An *application* (or *app*) is software that performs some useful task, such as writing a letter, sending email, or looking up information online. Windows comes with a variety of simple applications, and you can also acquire others.

Some applications have shortcut tiles pinned to the Start menu. These applications are easy to open;

just click the tile. If you want to open an application that does not have a pinned tile on the Start menu, you can click *All apps* to browse a list of installed applications and choose it from there. You can also click in the search box, start typing the name of the application, and then choose the application in the search results list.

Tutorial

3 *Another Way*
Press Alt + F4 to close almost any window.

TIP
The topmost button in the Photos app, called a *menu button* or a *hamburger button*, opens a menu. Clicking the same button again closes the menu.

Open and Close Applications from the Start Menu

1 Click the Start button.

2 Click the Photos tile.

3 Explore the Photos app by clicking the buttons along the left side.

4 Click the Close button to close the Photos window.

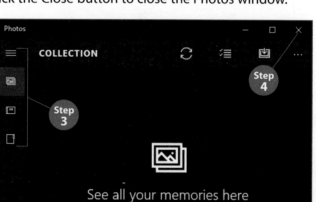

5 Click the Start button.

6 Click the All apps button.

7 Point to the right of the list of applications so that a scroll bar appears and then drag the scroll box downward until you see the *W* section.

TIP
The Paint application is useful for drawing pictures and making simple edits to photos.

8 Click *Windows Accessories* to expand that category.

9 Click *Paint*.

10–11 *Another Way*
Click the Close button to close the Paint window.

10 At the Paint window, click the File tab.

11 Click *Exit* to close the Paint window.

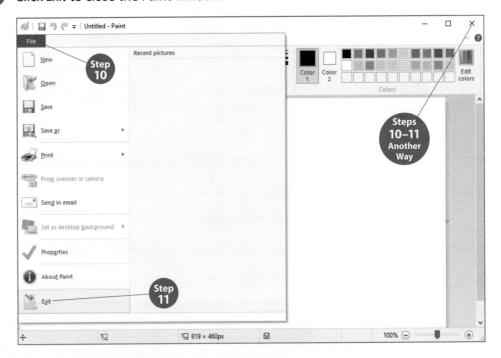

Open and Close Applications Using the Search Box

Tutorial

TIP

The first time you click in the search box after creating a new account, you might be asked a few questions. Respond to these before continuing.

12 On the Windows taskbar, click in the search box and then type note.

13 In the search results list, click *Notepad Desktop app*.

14 In the Notepad window, type your name.

15 Click the Close button to close the Notepad window.

16 Click the Don't Save button at the prompt asking if you want to save your work.

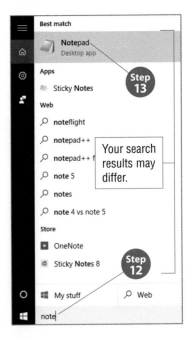

Your search results may differ.

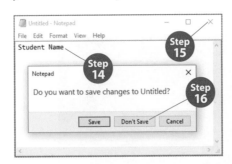

Online Extra

Skill Extra

Understanding Desktop and Modern Apps

Two types of applications run in Windows 10: desktop applications and Modern apps. A *desktop application* is designed to run on full-size desktop and laptop computers. Desktop applications have existed for decades. Examples include Notepad, Paint, and all the Microsoft Office applications. A *Modern app* is designed to run only on Windows 8 and higher. The Photos app you opened in this skill is an example. This type of application is typically simpler and uses less memory to run because it is created to run on almost any Windows 10 device, including tablets and smartphones.

Skill 4

Manipulate Windows

A *window* is a well-defined rectangular area onscreen in which an application runs, a file listing appears, or a message is displayed. As you saw in Skill 3, each application opens in its own window.

A window can appear in one of three states:

- *Maximized*: enlarged to fill the entire screen
- *Minimized*: open but temporarily hidden from view

- *Restored*: neither minimized nor maximized, and therefore able to be moved and resized

You can move and resize a window to meet the needs of the task you are performing. For example, if you have many windows open at once and you want to see all of them at a glance, you can make each window relatively small and arrange them side-by-side.

Tutorial

2 *Another Way*
Press Windows logo + Up Arrow.

1 On the Windows taskbar, click the File Explorer button to open the File Explorer application.

2 At the File Explorer window, click the Maximize button if the window is not already maximized. The window enlarges to fill the entire screen and the Maximize button changes to a Restore Down button.

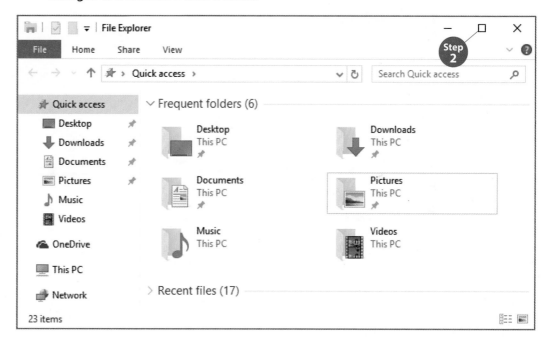

3, 4 *Another Way*
Press Windows logo + Down Arrow.

3 Click the Restore Down button. The window returns to its pre-maximized size and position and the Restore Down button changes to a Maximize button.

4 Click the Minimize button. The window disappears but the app is still running.

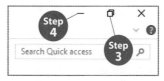

TIP

A colored line under a button on the Windows taskbar indicates the application is open.

5 On the Windows taskbar, click the File Explorer button. The File Explorer window returns to its pre-minimized state and position.

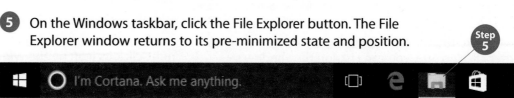

6 Point to the right border of the File Explorer window. The mouse pointer becomes a right-and-left-pointing arrow.

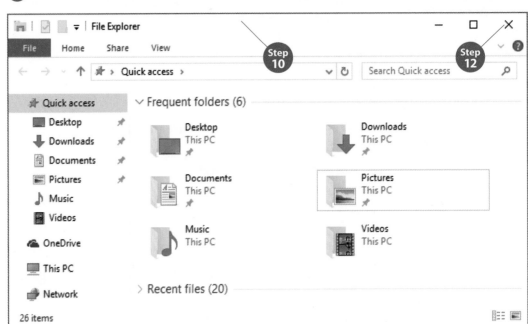

7 Drag the border to the right to enlarge the window horizontally.

8 Point to the lower right corner of the window. The mouse pointer becomes a diagonal two-headed arrow.

9 Drag the border down and to the left to make the window taller and narrower.

10 Point to the Title bar at the top of the window. The mouse pointer does not change in this case.

11 Drag the window to a different location on the desktop.

12 Click the Close button to close the File Explorer window.

TIP

Not all windows can be resized. Some applications have a fixed window size set by the programmers who created them.

⑫ Another Way

Press Alt + F4.

Skill Extras

Minimizing All Open Windows

Here's an easy way to minimize all windows at once. Click the Show Desktop button, which is the thin vertical bar to the right of the clock on the Windows taskbar. You can do the same thing by pressing Windows logo + M.

Using the Keyboard to Move and Resize Windows

If you right-click the Title bar on a window, you see a shortcut menu containing *Restore, Move, Size, Minimize, Maximize,* and *Close* options. After clicking *Move,* you can move the window using the arrow keys. Similarly, after clicking *Size,* you can change the window's dimensions using the arrow keys. Press Esc when finished moving or sizing.

Snapping Apps and Automatically Maximizing Windows

If you drag a Modern app window to the far right or left so it is at least halfway off the screen, and then drop it there, the window is resized and positioned to cover the right or left half of the screen. This is called snapping an app. If you drag a window up so its title bar touches the top of the screen, the window is automatically maximized.

Closing a Minimized Window

To close a minimized window without restoring it first, right-click its icon on the Windows taskbar and then click *Close window.*

Skill 5

Move between Open Windows

When multiple windows are open at once, you will likely want to switch between them. This is called *multitasking*. There are many different ways of doing so. By experimenting with the various methods, you can find the one you like best.

Tutorial

TIP

If the items in Steps 1–3 do not appear on your Windows taskbar, click any three buttons or icons of your choice.

TIP

You learned to size and move windows in Skill 4.

TIP

To move a maximized window, you must first restore it down by clicking its Restore Down button.

1 On the Windows taskbar, click the Microsoft Edge button to open the Microsoft Edge web browser. Restore the window down if it is maximized.

2 On the Windows taskbar, click the File Explorer button to open the File Explorer window. Restore the window down if it is maximized.

3 In the notification area of the Windows taskbar, right-click the speaker icon and then click *Sounds* to open the Sound dialog box.

4 If necessary, move the three open windows to arrange them so that at least a portion of each window is visible.

5 On the Windows taskbar, click the Sound button to switch to that window and make it active.

6 Click any visible portion of the File Explorer window to switch to that window.

7 Press the Alt key and hold it down while you press the Tab key repeatedly. You see a screen containing a thumbnail of each open window, with the currently selected window outlined.

8 Press the Tab key until the Microsoft Edge thumbnail is selected and then release the Alt key. The Microsoft Edge window becomes active.

9 On the Windows taskbar, click the Task View button. Thumbnail images of the open windows appear, similar to those in Steps 7–8, except these stay visible without your holding down any keys.

10 Click the File Explorer thumbnail to make the File Explorer window active.

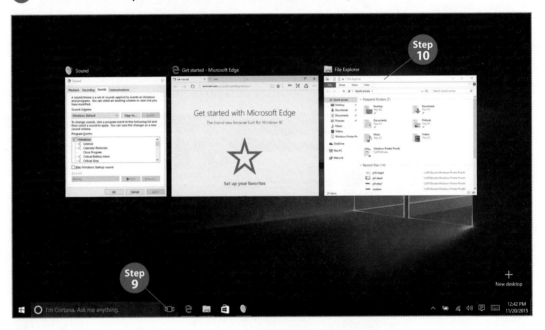

11 Press Alt + Esc to make a different window active.

13 Another Way
Press Alt + F4 three times.

12 Press Alt + Esc two more times, so that File Explorer is once again active.

13 Click the Close button on each open window to close the three open windows. When prompted as you close Microsoft Edge, click Close All Tabs.

Skill Extra

Working with Multiple Desktops

When you have many windows open at once, your desktop can get cluttered. If you want to start with a fresh-looking desktop without closing the open windows, you can create a new desktop. To do this, click the Task View button on the Windows taskbar and then click the New desktop button. Click anywhere in the new desktop to start working in it. To switch back to the original desktop, click the Task View button again and then click the thumbnail of the original desktop.

Skill 6

Work with Menus, Toolbars, Ribbons, and Dialog Boxes

Applications use a variety of interfaces to allow users to issue commands and make choices. Some apps (including Notepad and Windows Journal) use a *menu system*, in which a bar of menu names appears across the top of the window. The user clicks a menu name, a menu drops down, and the user clicks the desired option on the menu. Some menu-based applications also use a *toolbar*, which is a row of buttons (usually immediately below the menu bar), each representing a command. The user clicks the button to issue the desired command.

Instead of a menu system, other applications use a ribbon system. A *ribbon* is a toolbar with multiple tabs.

Each tab, when clicked, displays buttons and options the user can click to issue commands. In many cases, the buttons and options are organized in groups. Microsoft Office applications use a ribbon, as do File Explorer and many of the applications that come with Windows 10, like WordPad and Paint.

When clicked, some commands on menus, toolbars, and ribbons open dialog boxes. A *dialog box* is a window that asks the user for information. The user provides that information by clicking the controls in the dialog box and then clicking OK (or some similar command) to send the information back to the application that requested it.

Tutorial

TIP

If prompted to install a Journal Note Writer print driver in Step 2, click Cancel.

Use a Menu and Toolbar System

1. On the Windows taskbar, click in the search box and then type journal.

2. In the search results list, click *Windows Journal Desktop app* to open the application.

3. At the Windows Journal window, click *View* on the menu bar to open the View menu.

4. Point to the *Toolbars* command to display its menu. Do not click any options at the menu.

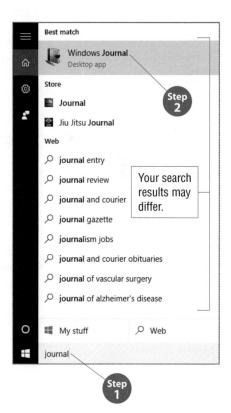

Your search results may differ.

TIP

If the File menu doesn't open when you point to *File* in Step 5, click *File*.

5. Point to *File* on the menu bar to open the File menu. Notice the *New Note* command with the Ctrl + N shortcut at the menu. Do not click the command.

6. Press the Esc key to close the menu and then press the Esc key again to deselect *File* on the menu bar.

TIP

Most toolbar buttons have menu equivalents, and some also have keyboard equivalents.

Tutorial

Tutorial

7 Point to the leftmost button on the toolbar so that a ScreenTip appears showing the button name: New Note. Do not click the button.

8 On the toolbar, click the *Page Width* box arrow to open a drop-down list. Click away from the list to close it without making a selection.

Use a Dialog Box

9 On the menu bar, click *Tools*.

10 At the menu that appears, click *Options*.

11 At the Options dialog box, confirm that the Note Format tab is active and then click the *Note template* option button to select it.

12 Click the *Stationery* option button to select it.

13 Click the View tab.

14 On the View tab, click the *Recently used folder list* increment (up) arrow twice to increase the value to 17.

15 Click the *Show as note titles* check box to remove the check mark.

16 Click the Cancel button to close the dialog box without saving your changes.

17 Click the Close button to close the Windows Journal application.

Use a Ribbon

18 On the Windows taskbar, click in the search box, type wordpad, and then click *WordPad Desktop app* in the search results list to open the application.

19 Click the View tab to see the commands on that tab.

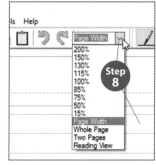

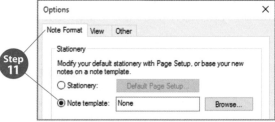

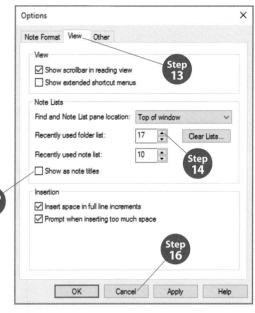

20 Click the Home tab to see the commands on that tab.

21 In the Paragraph group, point to the Align text left button to display its ScreenTip and then click the button to select it, if it is not already selected.

22 Click the Center button to select it. Notice that the Align text left button is no longer selected.

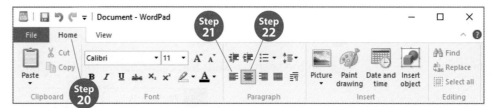

23 Click the File tab. The File tab is different from the other tabs; rather than displaying choices on the ribbon, it opens a menu.

24 Point to *Save as* and review the options at the submenu that opens. Do not click any of the options.

25 Click *Exit* to close WordPad. If prompted to save changes, click the Don't Save button.

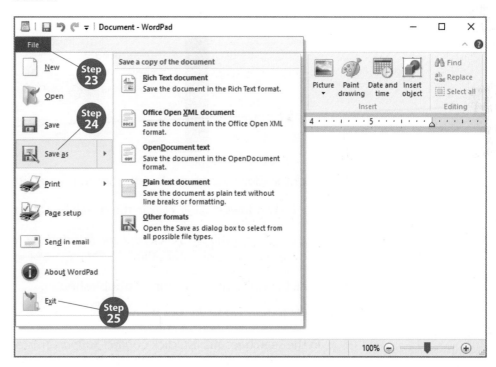

Online
Extras

Skill Extra

Using Contextual Tabs on a Ribbon

Certain ribbon tabs appear only when something triggers them in the application, such as when a certain kind of content is selected. This type of tab is called a *contextual tab*. For example, in File Explorer, when you have selected a picture file, the Picture Tools Manage tab is available. If you are following steps that ask you to select a particular ribbon tab that you don't see, check to make sure you have selected the object that would make that tab appear.

Get Help and Support in Windows

Windows 10 provides an entirely new way of accessing help information than did previous versions of Windows. Rather than providing a Help application, Windows 10 offers help and support information through the search box on the Windows taskbar. The search feature returns information from the Internet, from Cortana, and from the Windows help services.

Tutorial

1 On the Windows taskbar, click in the search box and then type time zone.

2 In the search results list, click *Change the Time Zone* to open the Settings app.

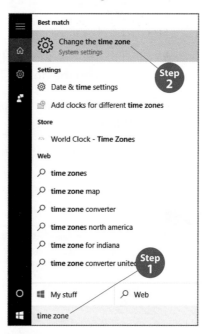

3 Click the Close button to close the Settings app without changing any settings.

4 On the Windows taskbar, click in the search box and then type troubleshoot printing.

5 In the search results list, click *Find and fix printing problems Control panel* to open the Printer troubleshooter utility.

6 Click Cancel to close the Printer troubleshooter.

TIP
In Step 6, if you were having a printer problem, you would click Next instead of Cancel and then work through the prompts in the troubleshooter.

7 Click in the search box and then type contact support.

8 In the search results list, click *Contact Support Trusted Windows Store app* to open the Contact Support application. Note that this application provides help with Microsoft accounts, services, and apps.

9 Click the Close button.

Skill Extra

Troubleshooting Wireless Network Problems
If you ever have a problem with your wireless network connection, here's an easy and direct way to start the network troubleshooter. Right-click the wireless networking icon in the notification area of the Windows taskbar and then click *Troubleshoot problems* at the shortcut menu.

Task Summary

Task	Button/Icon/Option	Action
close app	×	Click Close button. (Alternative methods: Press Alt + F4. *OR* Click File menu or tab, click *Exit*.)
display commands for feature in notification area		Right-click feature icon.
maximize window	□	Click Maximize button. (Alternative method: Press Windows logo + Up Arrow.)
minimize window	—	Click Minimize button. (Alternative method: Press Windows logo + Down Arrow.)
move desktop icon		Drag icon to desired location.
move window		Click Title bar and drag window to desired location.
open Start menu	⊞	Click Start button. (Alternative method: Press Windows logo key.)
resize window		Point to window border or corner until two-headed arrow appears, drag border or corner.
restore window	⧉	Click Restore Down button. (Alternative method: Press Windows logo + Down Arrow.)
search for app, feature, or help	○ I'm Cortana. Ask me anything.	On Windows taskbar, click in search box, type app or feature name or help topic, click match in search results list.
show hidden notification icons	⌃	In Windows taskbar notification area, click Show hidden icons button arrow.
sign in to Windows	Password →	Power up computer if needed, press any key or click to clear Lock screen if needed, type password in password box, press Enter.
sign out from Windows without shutting down	Sign out	Click Start button, click name of currently signed in user, click *Sign out*.
sign out from Windows and shut down	Shut down	Click Start button, click Power button, click *Shut down*.
start app from Start menu		Click Start button, click app shortcut or tile.
start app from Windows taskbar	e ▣ ▤	Click pinned button.
switch windows	⊡	On Windows taskbar, click Task View button, click app thumbnail. (Alternative methods: Click button on Windows taskbar. *OR* Press and hold Alt key, press Tab key until thumbnail is selected, release keys.)
use list box drop-down list	⌄	On toolbar or ribbon or in dialog box, click box arrow, click desired item at drop-down list.
use menu		Click menu name, point to command to display submenu if needed, click command.
use command buttons and check boxes		Click button or check box.
use ribbon		On ribbon, click desired tab. In group, click desired button or control.
use toolbar or Windows taskbar button		On toolbar or Windows taskbar, point to button to display ScreenTip, click button to issue command.

Recheck

Workbook

Chapter study tools, exercises, and assessments are available in the Workbook, which is accessed through your ebook.

Chapter 2

Precheck

Managing Files

In this chapter, you will learn how to use the Windows 10 File Explorer utility to locate files and perform common operations on them such as moving, copying, renaming, and deleting.

A *file* is a collection of data stored under a single name, such as MyLetter.docx. Most files have an *extension*, which is a period followed by a few letters or numbers. In the file name MyLetter.docx, *.docx* is the extension. The file extension tells Windows how to handle the file. Windows maintains a list of file extensions and which application handles them. For example, the *.docx* extension is assigned to Microsoft Word.

Files are stored locally on *volumes*. A volume is a storage location with a letter assigned to it, such as *C* or *D*. It might be a disk drive such as a hard disk, a removable disc such as a DVD, or a USB flash drive. Files can also be stored online, such as in a cloud service like OneDrive.

Within a volume, files are organized into logical groupings called *folders*. Folders typically have names that signal the purpose of the files stored within them, such as *Program Files*, *Users*, or *Downloads*. You can easily view different folders and browse their content in File Explorer, and search multiple folders for a specific file.

Sometimes groups of files are compressed into an archive file, which usually has a *.zip* extension. An archive file looks like one single file, and can be worked with as a single file, but it actually contains multiple files. It can be unpacked (decompressed) to extract the individual files within it. The data files for this textbook will come to you in a compressed archive, for example. You can also create your own compressed archives.

The File Explorer interface in Windows 10 makes it easy to select multiple files and then issue a command that affects all of them. For example, you can copy a group of files from your local hard drive to a USB flash drive to share with a friend. You can also delete files. A deleted file is not destroyed immediately; it is moved to the Recycle Bin. You can retrieve deleted files from the Recycle Bin if you change your mind about deleting them.

Skills You Learn

1 Navigate between Local Volumes and Folders in File Explorer

2 Control the Display of Hidden Files and File Extensions

3 Create and Rename a File or Folder

4 Download and Extract Student Data Files

5 Select Multiple Files and Folders

6 Create a Compressed Archive (ZIP) File

7 Move and Copy Files

8 Delete Files and Use the Recycle Bin

9 Search for a File

 SNAP If you are a SNAP user, go to your SNAP Assignments page to complete the Precheck, Tutorials, and Recheck.

Files You Use

In Skill 4 of this chapter, you will download the W10-StudentDataFiles folder and extract its contents to a USB flash drive. This folder contains the W10-Chapter2 folder, which holds the following data files needed for Skills 5–9 in this chapter:

W10-C2-Duncan.jpg
W10-C2-List.txt
W10-C2-Ring.jpg
W10-C2-Holiday Schedule.txt

Navigate between Local Volumes and Folders in File Explorer

File Explorer enables you to browse all the volumes and folders connected to your PC. These storage locations might include your PC's main hard disk drive, additional hard disk drives, optical discs such as CDs and DVDs, and USB flash drives. You can browse a volume's folders to find the file you want, or you can use shortcuts provided by Windows to browse specific locations such as Documents or Pictures.

The File Explorer window consists of two panes. On the left is the *Navigation pane*, containing shortcuts to make various locations active. On the right is the file list pane, showing the contents of whatever location is active. Across the top of the window is the *Address bar*, which reports the path of the active location—for example, This PC > Local Disk (C):.

Most people store most of their data files in one of the user folders that Windows 10 provides. On a Windows 10 computer, each user account has its own separate set of user folders, so each user's work remains private when multiple people share a computer. The shortcuts to locations such as Downloads, Pictures, and Music all point to the folders for the account of the user who is currently signed in. If a different user signs in, those shortcuts point to the corresponding folders for that different user.

The *Quick access list* displays by default at the top of the Navigation pane when you open File Explorer. It contains pinned shortcuts to user folders, and also shortcuts to recently used folders.

Tutorial

① Another Way
Click the Start button and then click *File Explorer*.

TIP
When a list is expanded, the arrow in front of it points down.

③ Another Way
In the Navigation pane, click the C: volume. You may need to scroll down to see it.

① On the Windows taskbar, click the File Explorer icon.

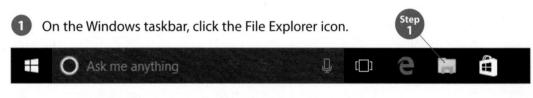

② In the Navigation pane, click *This PC* to select it. If you see a right-pointing arrow in front of it, click the arrow to expand the listing.

③ In the file list pane, double-click the C: volume.

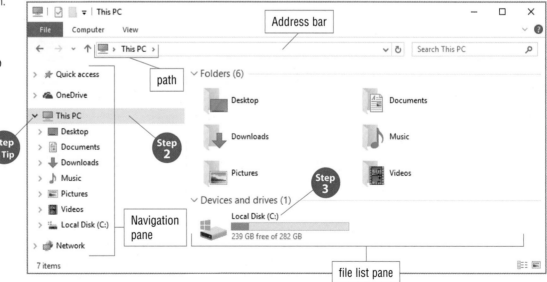

4 Double-click the *Program Files* folder.

5 *Another Way*
In the Address bar, click the
C: volume.

5 In the Address bar, click the Up arrow to go up one level, back to the top level folder of the C: volume.

6 In the Navigation pane, click *Documents* and note the contents displayed in the file list pane.

TIP
Clicking the Forward arrow will take you to the next viewed location.

7 In the Address bar, click the Back arrow to go back to the previous location.

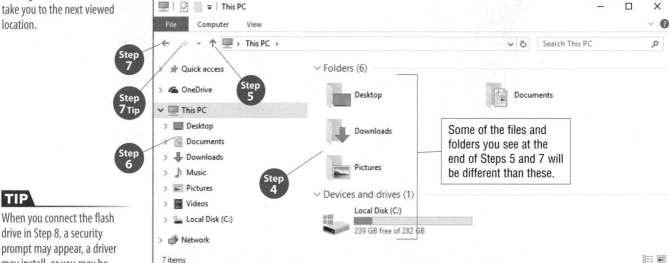

Some of the files and folders you see at the end of Steps 5 and 7 will be different than these.

TIP
When you connect the flash drive in Step 8, a security prompt may appear, a driver may install, or you may be asked to indicate what you want to do with the drive.

8 Connect a USB flash drive to the computer, and wait for it to appear in the Navigation pane under *This PC*. Depending on your settings, a new window may appear showing the contents of the flash drive.

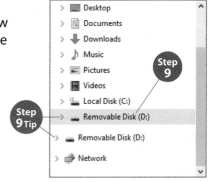

TIP
Your computer may display the USB flash drive with a name given to it by the manufacturer or user, or a generic name such as *Removable Disk*.

9 In the Navigation pane, click the USB flash drive to display its contents if they do not already appear.

TIP
The flash drive may appear twice in the Navigation pane, as shown here.

10 In the upper right corner of File Explorer, click the Close button. Repeat to close any additional File Explorer windows.

Online
Extras

11 Safely disconnect the USB flash drive from the computer. (See the Skill Extras for instructions on safely disconnecting the flash drive.)

Skill Extras

Safely Disconnecting a USB Device
If you disconnect a drive while file operations are still in progress, the file being written may be corrupted. To be sure all operations have completed, click the Safely Remove Hardware and Eject Media button in the notification area of the Windows taskbar and then click *Eject* at the shortcut menu. You can also right-click the drive in File Explorer and then click *Eject*.

Changing the Icon Size
On the View tab in File Explorer, use options in the Layout group to change the way a location's content is displayed. For example, the *Details* option displays files in columns containing information such as file name, size, type, and date. When you use the *Large icons* or *Extra Large icons* options, a file preview is displayed instead of a regular icon (if a file preview is available).

Skill 2

Control the Display of Hidden Files and File Extensions

In Windows, any file or folder can be marked as hidden. By default, File Explorer does not include hidden files and folders in listings, because presumably they are hidden for a good reason, such as to protect them. However, you may need to access hidden files or folders to make system changes. For example, you may need to access the AppData folder in your user account folder to modify themes or templates for an Office application. Windows allows you to change the default setting to show files and folders that are marked as hidden.

Each file name ends with a file extension (usually three or four characters) that indicates the file type. For example, *.exe* indicates an executable program file and *.txt* indicates a plain text file. By default, in File Explorer listings, Windows hides the extensions for file types that are registered in its database of file extensions and their assigned programs. When you are selecting files in File Explorer, you might want to see the extensions to better understand which files you are choosing. For example, if you had files named mortgage.txt and mortgage.xlsx, and file extensions were hidden, those two files would both appear as *mortgage* in the file listing. They would have different icons, but they would appear to have the same name.

Tutorial

1 *Another Way*
Click the Start button and then click *File Explorer*.

3 *Another Way*
In the Navigation pane, click the C: volume under *This PC*.

Show/Hide Hidden Files

1 On the Windows taskbar, click the File Explorer button.

2 In the Navigation pane, click *This PC*.

3 In the file list pane, double-click the C: volume.

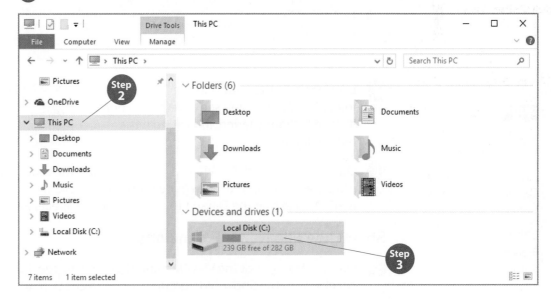

4 Double-click the *Users* folder in the file list pane. The content of that folder appears, with a folder for each user account on your PC. Make a note of the folders you see.

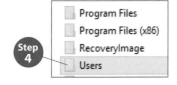

5 On the ribbon, click the View tab.

TIP

The folders you see in the Users folder correspond to the user accounts on the local PC. Depending on who uses your computer, you will have different account folders. Do not delete any of these folders, even if you don't recognize the user names.

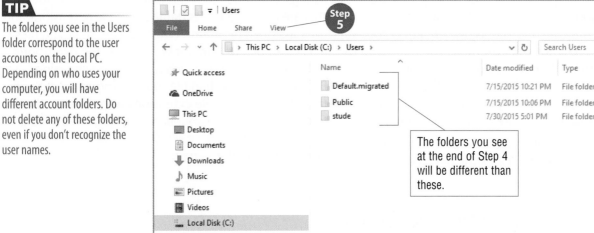

The folders you see at the end of Step 4 will be different than these.

6 Click the *Hidden items* check box in the Show/hide group to insert a check mark, if one does not already appear.

TIP

By default, none of the three check boxes in the Show/hide group contains a check mark. However, these settings may have been changed on your PC.

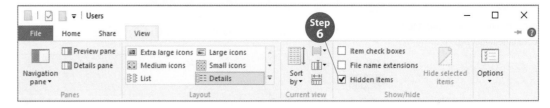

TIP

The File Explorer ribbon is collapsed by default. If you would like it to stay visible, follow the instructions in the Skill Extras at the end of these steps.

Tutorial

7 Look again at the folders in the Users folder listing. Now you see a Default folder. Its icon is slightly faded, indicating it is a hidden folder.

In Step 7, you see the Default folder with a faded icon.

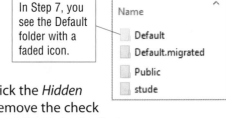

8 On the ribbon, click the View tab and then click the *Hidden items* check box in the Show/hide group to remove the check mark. Notice that the Default folder no longer appears in the listing.

Show/Hide File Name Extensions

9 On the ribbon, click the View tab and then look to see if the *File name extensions* check box in the Show/hide group contains a check mark. If it does, click the check box to remove the check mark.

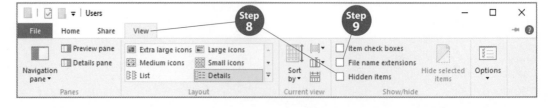

6 In File Explorer, click the Compressed Folder Tools Extract tab if necessary to make it active, and then click the Extract all button.

7 At the Extract Compressed (Zipped) Folders dialog box, click the Browse button and then navigate to your USB flash drive.

8 Click the Select Folder button to return to the Extract Compressed (Zipped) Folders dialog box.

9 Click the Extract button in the dialog box. The files are extracted and copied to your USB flash drive in a folder named W10-StudentDataFiles.

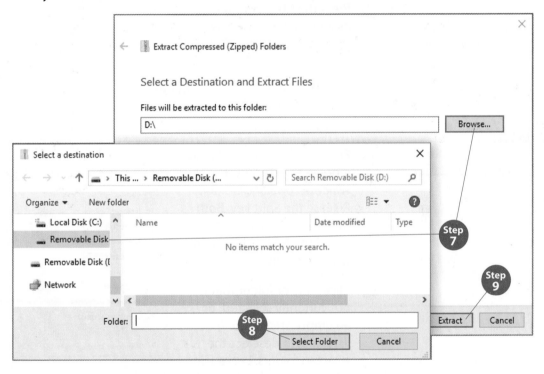

10 Close one File Explorer window and the OneDrive browser window. Leave the remaining File Explorer window open for the next skill.

11 Safely eject your USB flash drive.

Online
Extra

Skill Extra

Downloading Executable Files

Not every file you download will be a ZIP file. Some files you download will be executable files (with an *.exe* extension) that run programs when you double-click them. For example, you might download a setup program that installs or updates an application on your computer. Beware of downloading executable files from untrusted websites or unknown sources such as emails. They may contain viruses or other harmful software.

Select Multiple Files and Folders

Many actions, such as copying and deleting, can be performed on more than one file or folder at once. Before performing the action, you must make a multiple-item selection. All the items you select to be acted on as a group must be in the same location. For example, you can select a folder and three files that are all in the same folder, but you cannot select two files in different folders.

Tutorial

TIP

If you do not see the C: volume in Step 2, double-click *This PC* to expand the list.

TIP

Pressing Ctrl enables you to select multiple noncontiguous files or folders—that is, two or more files or folders that are not next to each other in a list.

TIP

You may need to scroll down in the file list pane to see the folders in Steps 5–7.

Online Extra

1 Open File Explorer if it is not already open.

2 In the Navigation pane, click the C: volume.

3 In the file list pane, double-click the *Program Files* folder to open it.

4 Click the *Common Files* folder to select it.

5 Press the Ctrl key and hold it down as you click the *Windows Mail* folder. Release the Ctrl key. Both folders are now selected.

6 Click the *Windows Defender* folder. The previously selected folders are now deselected.

7 Press the Shift key and hold it down as you click the *WindowsPowerShell* folder. Release the Shift key. Both folders are now selected, as are all the folders between them in the list.

8 Click a file or folder that is not currently selected, or an empty area of the file list pane, to deselect the selected folders. Leave File Explorer open for the next skill.

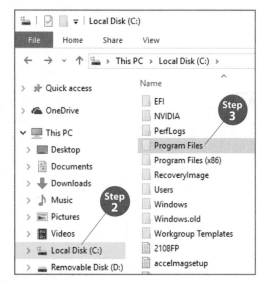

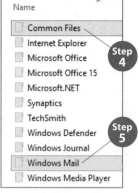

Skill Extra

Selecting Multiple Items with the Keyboard

You can also select multiple files and folders with the keyboard. To select noncontiguous items using the arrow keys: Highlight the first item you wish to select. Press the Ctrl key and hold it down while using the arrow keys to move to the next item, and then tap the spacebar to select the item. Continue pressing and holding the Ctrl key, and using the arrow keys and spacebar, until you have selected all the desired items. To select a contiguous block of items using the keyboard: Highlight the first item, and then press the Shift key and hold it down while using the arrow keys to extend the selection.

Skill 6

Create a Compressed Archive (ZIP) File

Windows makes it easy for you to create your own ZIP files. You might create a compressed archive file containing all your completed assignments for the week, for example, and then send that file to your instructor for grading. ZIP files simplify the process of transferring multiple files because they make it possible for you to work with the group as you would a single file.

Tutorial

TIP

Complete Skill 4 of this chapter if you have not yet downloaded the student data files to your USB flash drive.

1 Connect your USB flash drive containing the student data files.

2 Click the File Explorer button on the Windows taskbar to open File Explorer if it is not already open.

3 Double-click *This PC* in the Navigation pane if necessary to expand the list.

4 Click your USB flash drive in the Navigation pane.

5 In the file list pane, double-click the *W10-StudentDataFiles* folder to open it.

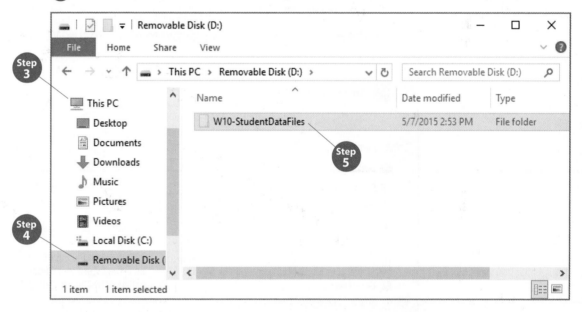

6 In the file list pane, double-click the *W10-Chapter2* folder to open it.

7 Select the four files in the *W10-Chapter2* folder.

TIP

See Skill 5 of this chapter for steps on selecting multiple files.

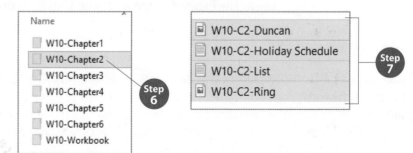

8–9 *Another Way*
Right-click the selected files, point to *Send to*, and then click *Compressed (zipped) folder*.

8. Click the Share tab on the ribbon.

9. Click the Zip button in the Send group.

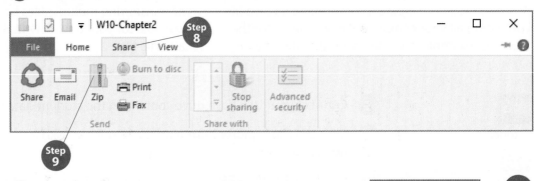

TIP
If you accidentally pressed Enter after Step 9, before you get a chance to rename the file in Step 10, press F2 to open the file name for editing.

10. Type W10-Chapter2-Skill6 and then press Enter to rename the new ZIP file.

11. Double-click the **W10-Chapter2-Skill6** file. Notice that all the files you selected in Step 7 appear inside it.

12. On the Address bar, click the Up arrow to return to the W10-Chapter2 folder.

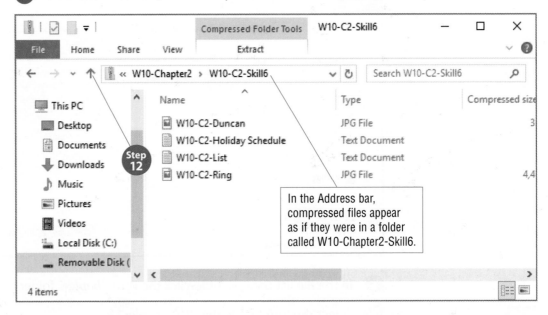

In the Address bar, compressed files appear as if they were in a folder called W10-Chapter2-Skill6.

13. Leave File Explorer open and your USB flash drive connected for the next skill.

Skill Extras

Using Other Types of Compressed Archives

ZIP files are by far the most common type of compressed archive on Windows systems, but other formats also exist. For example, TAR is the most popular format on Linux systems, and SIT (short for *StuffIt*) is popular on Mac. Windows users can open TAR and SIT files, as well as other compressed archive files, but a third-party utility program is required. WinZIP is one popular program you can use to open many different types of compressed archives.

Managing Compressed Archive Files

When you are viewing the contents of a compressed archive file, the Compressed Folder Tools Extract tab becomes available on the ribbon. To extract all the archive files to another location, click the Extract all button on this tab. To extract one or more individual files, select those files within the archive and then click one of the location shortcuts (such as *Documents* or *Desktop*) that appear in the Extract To group.

Skill 7
Move and Copy Files

You may sometimes need to move or copy data files between locations. For example, you might transfer a file from the Documents folder on your home computer to a USB flash drive to take it to school. Copying, as the name implies, leaves the file in its original location and places a copy of it in the destination location. Moving removes the file from the original location.

The two most common ways to move and copy files in Windows are to drag-and-drop and to use the Windows Clipboard. When you *drag-and-drop* files, both the original location and the destination must be visible in File Explorer. The destination can be visible as a separate File Explorer window or as a shortcut in the Navigation pane. If the original location and the destination are on the same volume, the default is a move operation. If they are not on the same volume, the default is a copy

operation. You can force a move operation regardless of the default by pressing Shift as you drag, or force a copy operation by pressing Ctrl as you drag.

The *Clipboard* is a temporary holding area in memory. When you select a file and then issue the Cut or Copy command, the selection is either moved or copied to the Clipboard. You then display the destination location and issue the Paste command to complete the operation.

Your hard disk contains both data files and program files. A *data file* is a file you create in an application to store your work; a *program file* is a file that runs a program. You should move only data files, not program files. If you move a program file, or any of its helper files, the program might not run correctly.

Tutorial

Move and Copy Using Drag-and-Drop

1 Make sure your USB flash drive containing the student data files is connected and File Explorer is open.

2 In the Navigation pane, click the USB flash drive to display its contents.

3 Right-click the USB flash drive to display a shortcut menu.

4 Click *Open in new window* at the shortcut menu. A new File Explorer window opens, showing the same location.

TIP
See Chapter 1, Skill 4, if you need help sizing and arranging windows.

5 Size and arrange the windows so they are side by side and the file list panes of both windows are visible.

6 In the file list pane of the left window, double-click the *W10-StudentDataFiles* folder.

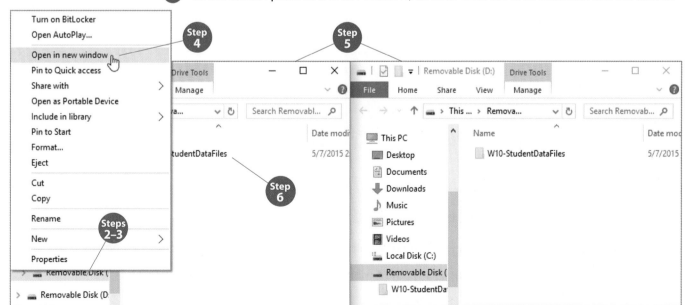

TIP

When locations are on the same volume, dragging-and-dropping moves the folder.

⑦ In the Navigation pane of the right window, click the *Documents* folder.

⑧ Drag-and-drop the W10-Chapter2 folder from the file list pane in the left window to the file list pane in the right window. Because the locations are on different volumes, dragging-and-dropping copies the folder.

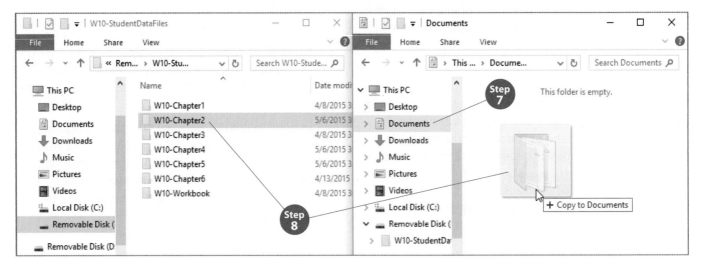

Move and Copy Using Copy and Paste

Tutorial

⑨ In the Navigation pane of the right window, click the USB flash drive to redisplay its contents.

⑩ On the Quick Access Toolbar of the right window, click the New folder button to create a new folder.

⑪ Type W10-Backup.

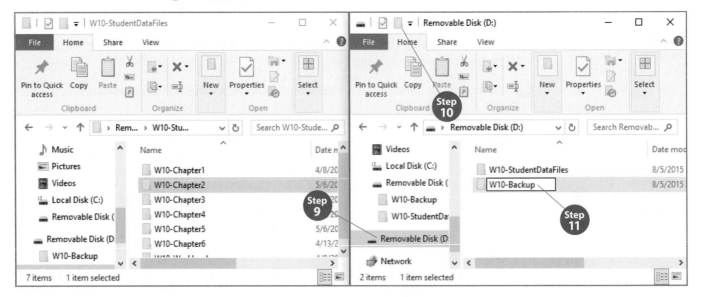

⑫ Press Enter.

⑬ Double-click the new folder to open it. Notice that it is currently empty.

⑭ In the file list pane of the left window, double-click the *W10-Chapter2* folder to open it.

15 Click the ***W10-C2-Ring*** file.

16 Click the Home tab and then click the Copy button in the Clipboard group.

17 Click the right window to make it active, click the Home tab, and then click the Paste button in the Clipboard group. The copied file is pasted from the Clipboard into the W10-Backup folder.

18 Close the left window (the W10-Chapter2 window).

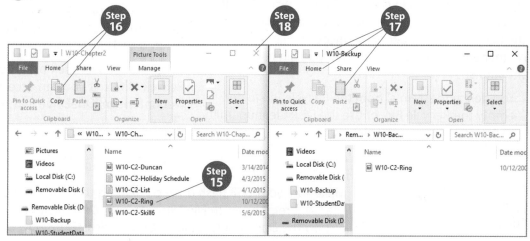

19 In the Navigation pane of the remaining File Explorer window, click the USB flash drive to return to its top level.

20 Click the *W10-Backup* folder, if it is not already selected.

21 On the Home tab, click Copy.

22 In the Navigation pane, click *Documents*.

23 On the Home tab, click Paste. Leave your USB flash drive connected and File Explorer open for the next skill.

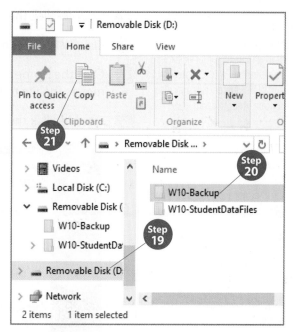

Skill Extras

Using the Move To and Copy To Buttons
On the Home tab of the ribbon, you'll find buttons that provide an alternative way to move and copy. To move a file, click the file to select it, click the Home tab, click the Move to button in the Organize group, and then click the desired location at the shortcut menu. If you don't see the location you want at the shortcut menu, click *Choose location*, browse to the desired location at the dialog box, and then click the Move button.

Working with Navigation Pane Locations
If the desired destination location appears as an icon on the Navigation pane, you can drag-and-drop a file or folder onto that icon to move or copy it to that destination. The shortcuts in the Quick access list on the Navigation pane are especially useful, because they include folders you have used recently or frequently.

Skill 8

Delete Files and Use the Recycle Bin

To save storage space and keep your files organized, you might delete some files. For example, when you are finished with this textbook, you might delete the student data files that you downloaded. Even after a file or folder has been deleted, you might be able to get it back. On volumes that are protected by the Recycle Bin, deleted files are stored in a system folder called Recycle Bin. Once a file has been deleted from the Recycle Bin, it is permanently gone. Files are permanently deleted from the Recycle Bin in these situations:

- You delete the item(s) from the Recycle Bin folder, empty the Recycle Bin, or use the Disk Cleanup utility to remove unnecessary files.

- The Recycle Bin exceeds its preset size limit, or the hard disk on which it is stored becomes nearly full. In either case, Windows automatically deletes files from the Recycle Bin, beginning with the oldest files.

The Recycle Bin does not protect external drives, such as USB flash drives, or drives that you access via the Internet or your local area network. When you delete files from those locations, they are permanently deleted and cannot be retrieved.

OneDrive file storage has its own separate online Recycle Bin that you can access via OneDrive's web interface. OneDrive features are discussed in Chapter 4.

Tutorial

TIP

The Documents folder contains at least three folders that you placed there in earlier skills: W10-Backup, W10-Chapter2, and W10-Reference. It may also contain other folders.

3–4 *Another Way*
Right-click the file and then click *Delete*.
OR
Click the file and then press the Delete key.

TIP

If you are prompted for confirmation when you click Delete in Step 4, see the Skill Extra section following these steps.

TIP

Your Recycle Bin might contain other files besides W10-C2-Ring. You may need to scroll to locate the file.

1 Make sure your USB flash drive containing the student data files is connected and File Explorer is open. In File Explorer, click *Documents* in the Navigation pane to display the Documents folder if it is not already displayed.

2 Double-click the *W10-Backup* folder to display its contents.

3 Click *W10-C2-Ring*.

4 Click the Home tab and then click the Delete button in the Organize group. This moves the file to the Recycle Bin.

5 Double-click the Recycle Bin icon on the desktop to open the Recycle Bin window.

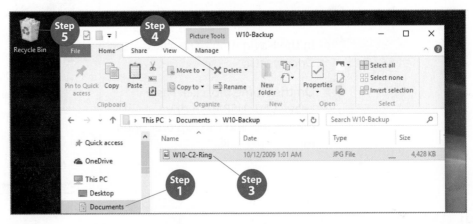

6 In the Recycle Bin window, click *W10-C2-Ring* to select it.

7 On the Recycle Bin Tools Manage tab, click the Restore the selected items button in the Restore group. The file returns to its original location in the W10-Backup folder.

8 Click the W10-Backup window to make it active, and then click *Documents* in the Navigation pane to return to that folder.

9 In the file list pane, click the *W10-Backup* folder, if it is not already selected, and then press Ctrl and click the *W10-Reference* folder. Both folders are selected.

10 On the Home tab, click the Delete button to move those folders to the Recycle Bin.

⑪ *Another Way*
Right-click the Recycle Bin icon on the desktop, and then click *Empty Recycle Bin*.

11 Click the Recycle Bin window to make it active, and then, on the Recycle Bin Tools Manage tab, click the Empty Recycle Bin button in the Manage group.

12 At the Delete Multiple Items dialog box, click Yes to confirm. Everything in the Recycle Bin is permanently deleted.

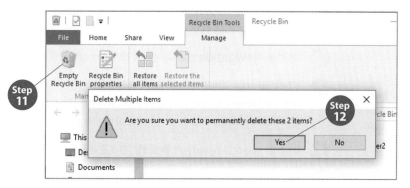

13 Close the Recycle Bin window.

14 In the Navigation pane of the remaining File Explorer window, click your USB flash drive to display its contents.

15 In the file list pane, click the *W10-Backup* folder and then press the Delete key.

TIP
When you try to delete a file from your USB flash drive in Step 16, a confirmation box appears because the Recycle Bin does not protect external drives.

16 Click Yes to confirm the deletion.

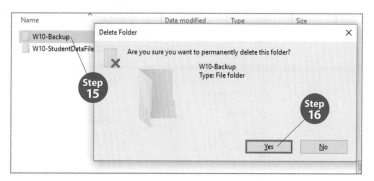

Online
Extras

17 Safely disconnect your USB flash drive from the PC. Leave File Explorer open for the next skill if it doesn't close automatically.

Skill Extra

Turning Off Deletion Confirmations

If you see a confirmation box asking if you want to permanently delete a deleted item or items, as you did in Steps 12 and 16 of this skill, it means that the location from which you are deleting is not protected by the Recycle Bin. On the other hand, if you see a confirmation box asking if you want to move the item or items to the Recycle Bin, it means that deletion confirmation is enabled. To turn off deletion confirmation, on the ribbon, click the Home tab, click the Delete button arrow, and then click *Show recycle confirmation* at the drop-down list.

Skill 9
Search for a File

If you forget where a file or folder is stored, or even what you named it, you might remember certain other details such as the type of file it was, a word or phrase that it contained, or the date it was last modified. Windows enables you to search for a file by using any of several criteria.

There are two ways to search for a file in Windows: by using the search box in File Explorer or by asking Cortana for help. *Cortana* is the integrated search assistant for Windows 10, and it searches both your local computer and the Internet. You will learn more about Cortana in Chapter 3.

Tutorial

TIP

Navigating to a certain location, as you do in Step 2, confines the search to that location and its subfolders. This can make the search run faster.

Search with the File Explorer Search Box

1 Open File Explorer if it is not already open. If there is a flash drive connected to the PC, disconnect it.

2 In the Navigation pane, click *Documents*.

3 Click in the File Explorer search box and then type List. The search begins immediately, listing all the files in the Documents folder that contain the word *List* in their names. Wait for the search to complete.

4 In the search results, click **W10-C2-List**.

5 On the ribbon, click the Search Tools Search tab and then click the Open file location button in the Options group. File Explorer switches to show the contents of the W10-Chapter2 folder and the Search Tools Search tab disappears.

TIP

If you have completed the previous skills in this chapter, the search results in Step 4 will include the files shown here.

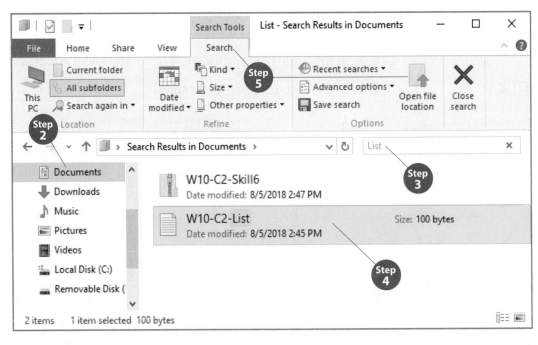

Skill Extra

Searching Inside Files

To speed up searches and eliminate many false positives, Windows does not look inside a file when performing a search with File Explorer. For example, if a text file named Vacation.txt contains the word *holiday*, a search for the word *holiday* will not find that

file. However, you can configure Search to look inside files as needed. On the Search Tools Search tab, click the Advanced Options button arrow and then click *File contents* at the drop-down list to toggle on that option. Repeat the same sequence of steps to toggle the option off again when you are finished with your search.

TIP

When you search in a particular location, the results list will not include files and folders located elsewhere, even if their names contain the search word.

TIP

In Step 7, the Address bar shows a green progress bar while the search is in progress. When the Address bar returns to white, the search is complete. You do not have to wait for the search to complete before continuing to Step 8.

6 In the File Explorer search box, type Windows. No search results are found because you are currently searching only within the W10-Chapter2 folder.

7 Click the Search Tools Search tab and then click the This PC button in the Location group. The search reruns, searching the entire PC rather than just the W10-Chapter2 folder. This time, many results are found.

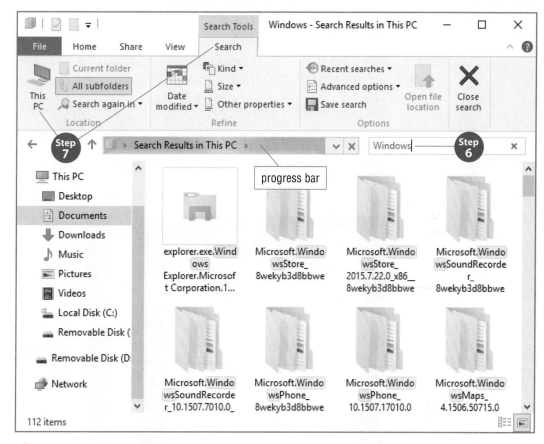

8 Click the Search Tools Search tab, and then click the Kind button arrow in the Refine group.

9 Click *Folder* at the drop-down list. The search results are filtered to show only folders with *Windows* in their names.

10 Close File Explorer.

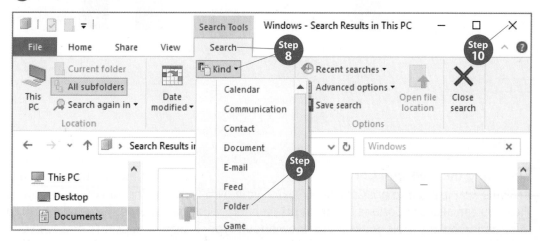

Tutorial

TIP

You do not have to wait for Cortana to finish searching before going on to Step 12.

Search with Cortana

11 Click in the search box on the Windows taskbar and then type W10-C2-Duncan. Cortana displays the search results.

12 At the top of the results list, click **W10-C2-Duncan.jpg** *JPG File View photo*. The picture opens in the Photos app.

13 Close the Photos app.

14 Click in the search box on the Windows taskbar and then type W10-C2-Duncan again. Cortana displays the search results again.

15 At the bottom of the search results pane, click *My stuff*.

16 View the search results in the expanded search results pane.

17 Point to the found picture to see its location in a ScreenTip.

18 Click away from the search results pane to close it.

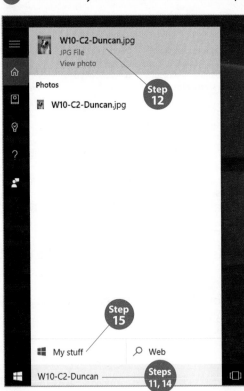

Skill Extra

Searching the Web with Cortana

In Skill 9, you learned to use Cortana to search your own files. You can also use Cortana to search the web for information on any topic you want to know about. Type a term or phrase describing the topic in the search box on the Windows taskbar, and then click *Web* to search online (instead of clicking *My stuff* in the search results list to search your own files). You will learn more about searching using Cortana in Chapter 3.

Task Summary

Task	Button/Icon/Option	Action
close File Explorer	×	In upper right corner of File Explorer, click Close button.
copy and paste files using Clipboard	Copy Paste	In File Explorer window, select files, click Copy button in Clipboard group on Home tab, go to destination folder, click Paste button.
copy files using drag-and-drop	+ Copy to Documents	In File Explorer, open windows for source and destination volume folders, select files in source folder, drag files to destination folder.
create and name ZIP file	Zip	In file list pane of File Explorer window, select files. On Share tab, click Zip button in Send group, type name, press Enter.
create and name new file		In file list pane of File Explorer window, right-click a blank area, point to *New*, click document type, type name, press Enter.
create and name new folder		On Quick Access Toolbar in File Explorer window, click New folder button, type name, press Enter.
delete file	Delete	In file list pane of File Explorer window, click Home tab, click Delete button in Organize group.
empty Recycle Bin	Recycle Bin	On desktop, double-click Recycle Bin icon. In Recycle Bin window, click Recycle Bin Tools Manage tab, click Empty Recycle Bin button in Manage group, close Recycle Bin window.
expand or collapse Navigation pane item	> ∨	In Navigation pane of File Explorer window, click right-pointing arrow next to item to expand listing or down-pointing arrow to collapse it.
go backward, forward, and up one level in folder structure	← → ↑	In Address bar of File Explorer window, click Back arrow to go to previous location, click Forward arrow to go to next location, click Up arrow to go up one level.
move files using drag-and-drop		Open separate File Explorer windows for source folder in one volume and destination folder in another volume, select files in source folder, press and hold Shift key while dragging files to destination folder.
open File Explorer		On Windows taskbar, click File Explorer button.
rename file or folder	Rename	In File Explorer window, click file or folder, click Rename button in Organize group on Home tab (or press F2), type new name, press Enter.
restore file from Recycle Bin	Restore the selected items	On desktop, double-click Recycle Bin icon. In Recycle Bin window, click file, click Recycle Bin Tools Manage tab, click Restore the selected items button in Restore group, close Recycle Bin window.
search for file using File Explorer	Search Documents 🔍	In Navigation pane of File Explorer window, click storage location to search, click in File Explorer search box, type file name.
select multiple contiguous files		In file list pane of File Explorer window, click first file, press and hold Shift key, click last file, release Shift key.
select multiple noncontiguous files		In file list pane of File Explorer window, click first file, press and hold Ctrl key, click additional files, release Ctrl key.
show/hide file name extensions and/or hidden items	☐ File name extensions ☐ Hidden items	On ribbon in File Explorer window, click View tab, click *File name extensions* and/or *Hidden items* check boxes in Show/hide group.
unpack ZIP file	Extract all	In File Explorer window, select file, click Compressed Folder Tools Extract tab, click Extract all button, select folder, click Extract button.

Recheck

Workbook

Chapter study tools, exercises, and assessments are available in the Workbook, which is accessed through your ebook.

Chapter 3

Precheck

Getting Information from the Internet

The heart of the Internet is a system of interconnected file servers called the *worldwide web* (or *web*). Web servers store individual data files called *web pages*, each of which has a unique address, called a *uniform resource locator (URL)*. If you know a web page's URL, you can view that page using *web browser* software on almost any computing device. A collection of related pages is known as a *website*.

Windows 10 comes with the *Microsoft Edge* browser, which replaces Internet Explorer (IE), Microsoft's browser from earlier Windows versions. You can access the web with a different browser, such as Google Chrome or Mozilla Firefox, if you like. However, because Microsoft Edge comes with Windows, it is the browser you will learn about in this chapter.

Skills You Learn

1 Get Started with the Microsoft Edge Browser

2 Use Tabbed Browsing

3 Use Search Engines to Find Content

4 Download a File from a Website

5 Save and Reopen Favorites

6 Review Browser History and Clear Browsing Data

7 Print a Web Page

8 Use Cortana to Get Information Online

 SNAP If you are a SNAP user, go to your SNAP Assignments page to complete the Precheck, Tutorials, and Recheck.

Files You Use

For these skills, you do not need any student data files.

Get Started with the Microsoft Edge Browser

The Microsoft Edge browser is the default browser in Windows 10, so when you click a link in a document or email message, the web page opens in Microsoft Edge. You can also launch Microsoft Edge from its button on the Windows taskbar or from its shortcut on the Start menu.

The Microsoft Edge interface is very spare and clean compared to most web browsers. Just a few buttons appear on a simple toolbar, and a search box and an Address bar allow you to type URLs for the pages you want to visit and locate information on any topic.

Even though Microsoft Edge is the primary browser in Windows 10, Internet Explorer remains available, and any pages that Microsoft Edge cannot load will open automatically in Internet Explorer.

Tutorial

1 Another Way
On the Windows taskbar, click in the search box, type Microsoft Edge, and then click *Microsoft Edge Microsoft recommended browser* in the search results list.

TIP

The protocol (e.g., *http://*) may not appear in the Address bar because Microsoft Edge simplifies the display. Click in the Address bar to see the full address.

1 On the Windows taskbar, click the Microsoft Edge button to start the Microsoft Edge browser.

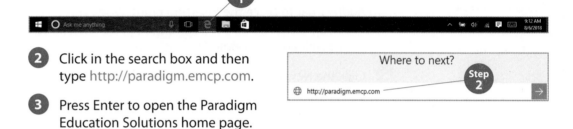

2 Click in the search box and then type http://paradigm.emcp.com.

3 Press Enter to open the Paradigm Education Solutions home page.

4 In the navigation bar on the web page, point to *About* and then click *Company Info* at the drop-down menu to view the Company Info page on the same website.

5 Click the Back arrow to return to the previously viewed page—in this case, the Paradigm Education Solutions home page.

6 Click the Forward arrow to go forward to view the Company Info page again.

7 Click the Refresh button to reload the page. Leave Microsoft Edge open for the next skill.

Skill Extra

Navigating in Other Browsers

Windows 10 allows you to download and run other web browsers. The most popular alternatives for Windows users are Google Chrome and Mozilla Firefox.

Microsoft's earlier browser, Internet Explorer, is also available in Windows 10. Each of these browsers has the same navigation features as Microsoft Edge, including Back, Forward, and Refresh buttons.

Skill 2

Use Tabbed Browsing

With Microsoft Edge, and most other modern browsers, you can have more than one web page open at once, each on its own tab in the browser window. You can click a tab to switch to that page, or close a tab when you are finished working with it.

Tutorial

TIP

If you do not see the Address bar in Step 1, click where it should be (see Step 3) or click in the search box (see Step 5).

1 With Microsoft Edge open, click in the Address bar, type https://www.microsoft.com/en-us/default.aspx, and then press Enter.

2 Click the New tab button to open a new browser tab.

3 Click in the blank area below the tabs to display the Address bar, click in the Address bar to place the insertion point, type https://www.google.com/chrome/browser/desktop/index.html, and then press Enter to open a page from which you can download the Google Chrome browser.

4 Click the New tab button to open another new tab.

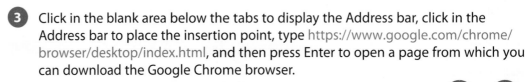

5 Type https://www.firefox.com in the search box, and then press Enter to open the Mozilla Firefox home page.

TIP

Don't worry that what you typed in Step 5 is not what appears in the Address bar. Many sites redirect your request to other pages, as explained in the Skill Extra at the end of these steps.

6 *Another Way*
Press Ctrl + W.

6 Click the Close button to close the Download Firefox — Free tab.

The URL you type in Step 5 redirects to this address.

7 Right-click the Chrome Browser tab and then click *Duplicate tab* at the shortcut menu. Now there are two identical Chrome Browser tabs.

8 Right-click the new Chrome Browser tab and then click *Close other tabs* at the shortcut menu to close all the other tabs. Leave Microsoft Edge open for the next skill.

Online Extras

Skill Extra

Understanding Redirects

When you type a URL, the website may redirect you to a different address. Websites use redirects for many different reasons. For example, when you type https://www.firefox.com, you are redirected to https://www.mozilla .org, which is the website for the parent company of the Mozilla Firefox browser. Some websites redirect to different versions depending on the browser you are using; for example, you may be redirected to a version optimized for viewing on a smartphone.

Skill 3
Use Search Engines to Find Content

Sometimes you might have a URL to manually type into the Address bar to open a particular site, but more often you will not know the exact URL for the content you want to see. You can use a search engine to search the Internet for what you want. A *search engine* is a website or service that is dedicated to maintaining a searchable directory of web content. To use a search engine, you can navigate to its website and type keywords in the search box. Most browsers are allied with a particular search engine. For example, when you type in the Microsoft Edge search box, the browser uses the Microsoft search engine, Bing. However, you can use any search engine with any browser. To use another search engine, navigate to its website and then type keywords in the search box at that site.

Tutorial

TIP

Your search results will likely be different from what is shown here, because the Internet and the search engine results are constantly changing.

1 With Microsoft Edge open, click in the Address bar, type MLA research paper, and then press Enter to display the search results.

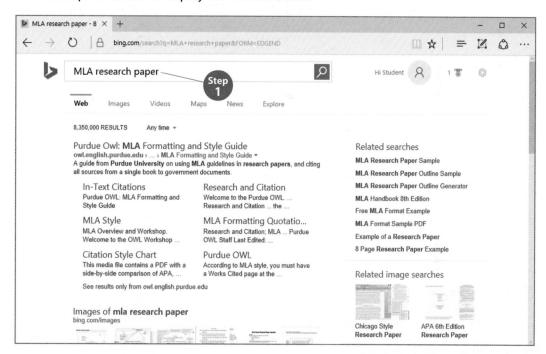

TIP

If Microsoft Edge tries to auto-complete the address with extra text in Step 2, press the space bar once after typing https://www.google.com but before pressing Enter.

2 Click in the Address bar, type https://www.google.com, and then press Enter to open the Google search engine home page.

TIP

As you type in the search box in Step 3, a list of suggestions appears. You can stop typing and click your search term in this list if it appears.

TIP

Your search results may be different from the ones shown here.

3 Click in the search box and then type MLA research paper. When you begin typing, the display immediately switches to a search results page.

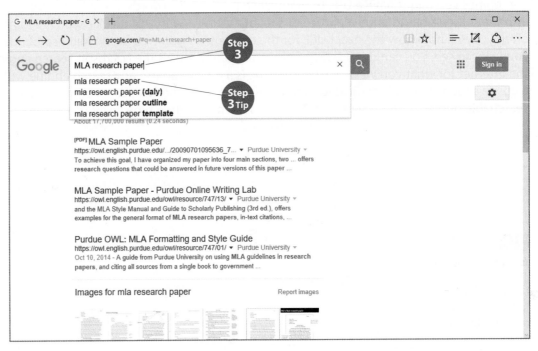

4 In the search results, click any item that interests you to display that page. Leave Microsoft Edge open for the next skill.

Skill Extras

Zooming In and Out on a Web Page

You can use Zoom to change the magnification at which web content is displayed. Click the More actions button (...) in the upper right corner of the Microsoft Edge window to open a drop-down menu. At the menu, click the minus sign (−) next to Zoom to zoom out, or the plus sign (+) to zoom in. Zooming in usually makes the text and graphics on the page appear larger, and zooming out usually makes them appear smaller. Zooming doesn't always work on every page because some pages are coded to always display items at a certain size regardless of the browser's settings.

Trying Out Other Popular Search Engines

Here are a few popular search engines. Try the same search in several different search engines to see if you get different results.

Dogpile (http://www.dogpile.com)
Goodsearch (http://www.goodsearch.com)
Yahoo! (https://www.yahoo.com)

Skill 4
Download a File from a Website

Not all hyperlinks open web pages. Some of them initiate file downloads when you click them. When you download a file with Microsoft Edge, the downloaded file is placed in your personal Downloads folder

(C: > Users > *username* > Downloads where *username* is your account). After the download has completed, you can use the Downloads list in Microsoft Edge to access your downloaded file.

Tutorial

1 With Microsoft Edge open, click in the Address bar, type http://W10.ParadigmCollege.net/Riley, and then press Enter to open the Agility Trial Champion web page.

2 In the *To download Riley's pedigree information* line, click the <u>click here</u> hyperlink.

Agility Trial Champion

On April 14th, at the Central Indiana Agility Club trial at the Hamlilton County Fairgrounds, my dog Riley (*Phantasm's Life of Riley*) completed the requirements for Canine Performance Events (CPE) Agility Trial Champion (C-ATCH) and was awarded a certificate and ribbon.
For more information about CPE, <u>click here</u>. **Step 2**

To download Riley's pedigree information, <u>click here</u>.

TIP
You can click the file in the Downloads list to open it in its native application. For example, the pedigree.xlsx file opens in Microsoft Excel, if that application is installed on your PC.

3 Wait for the file to finish downloading and then click the View downloads button to display the Downloads list.

Step 3

| pedigree.xlsx finished downloading. | Open | Open folder | View downloads | ✕ |

4 Press Esc to close the Downloads list.

5 Click the Hub button to open the Hub.

6 Click the Downloads button to open the Downloads list if it does not already appear.

7 Click anywhere on the web page outside the Downloads list to close it. Leave Microsoft Edge open to the Agility Trial Champion web page for the next skill.

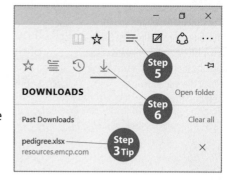

Online
Extra

Skill Extra

Reducing the Risk of Malware in Downloads
Be cautious when downloading files from websites. Most downloaded data files (pictures, documents, and so on) are fine. However, a downloaded executable file might contain *malware* that could harm your system or install nuisance software that displays ads. Generally, you should download executable files only from websites that you know and trust.

Skill 5

Save and Reopen Favorites

You can save the URLs of pages you want to visit again later, and then choose them from a list in your browser. The names used for the list and its items vary depending on your browser. Microsoft Edge calls it the *Favorites list* and calls each item a *favorite*. Most other browsers call it the *Bookmark list* and call individual items on the list *bookmarks*.

The items you add to your Favorites list are associated with your Windows user account. This means that anyone else signing into the same computer using a different account will not see your items but will instead see their own.

Tutorial

TIP

If the Agility Trial Champion web page is not open when you start this skill, repeat Skill 4, Step 1 to open it.

TIP

The active pane in Step 2 is whichever pane was most recently selected.

1. With Microsoft Edge open to the Agility Trial Champion web page, click the Add to favorites or reading list button to open the Add to Favorites or Reading list pane.

2. If needed, click the Favorites button at the top of the pane so that it is selected (blue and underlined).

3. Type Riley's Award to replace the text that appears in the *Name* box by default.

4. Click the *Create in* box arrow and then click *Favorites* at the drop-down list, if it is not already selected.

5. Click the Add button.

6. Click in the Address bar, type http://paradigm.emcp.com, and then press Enter.

7. Click the Hub button.

TIP

The Hub button allows you to manage your favorites, reading list, history, and downloads. Use the four buttons across the top of the Hub to switch between these categories.

8. If needed, click the Favorites button at the top of the Hub to display the Favorites list.

9. Click *Riley's Award* in the Favorites list to reopen that page. Leave Microsoft Edge open for the next skill.

Online Extras

Skill Extra

Saving to the Favorites Bar

Clicking *Favorites* at the *Create in* drop-down list saves an item to the Favorites list. Clicking *Favorites Bar* at the drop-down list saves the item to the Favorites bar, which is a toolbar below the Address bar in the Microsoft Edge window. The advantage of saving an item to the Favorites bar is that the shortcut will be available as a button there, without requiring you to open a menu. The disadvantage is that there is space for only a limited number of buttons to appear on the Favorites bar at once.

Review Browser History and Clear Browsing Data

The *browser history* is a list of all the sites you have recently visited. You can use it to return to recent pages quickly, even if you did not mark them as favorites.

A *cookie* is a small text file that a website might save to your hard drive to help remember your settings when you visit the same page again. For example, a cookie might remember the content of your shopping cart or what country you are in. Some advertisers also use cookies to track your shopping and browsing habits.

For privacy, you can clear your browsing data, including history and cookies, so that nobody else using your computer can see what sites you have visited.

Tutorial

In Steps 3–4, if you don't see *Google* in the History list, click the *Today* heading to expand that section. If you still don't see *Google*, scroll down in the History list.

Tutorial

Review Browser History

1 With Microsoft Edge open, click the Hub button.

2 Click the History button to open the History list.

3 Point to *Google* so that an X appears to its right.

4 Click the X to remove that item.

5 Click one of the remaining items in the History list to redisplay its page.

Clear Browsing Data

6 Click the More actions button (…) to open a menu.

7 At the menu, click *Settings* to open the SETTINGS pane.

8 In the *Clear browsing data* section, click the Choose what to clear button.

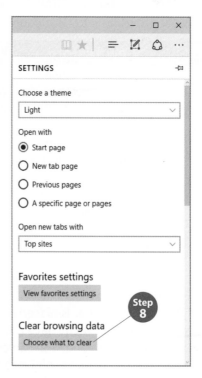

TIP

For additional types of data in Step 9, click *Show more*.

TIP

If you are using your own PC, you might not want to clear passwords and form data because it is useful to have that information fill in automatically. If you are using a public or school computer, you should clear that data to protect your privacy.

9 For each type of data listed, click to insert a check mark if you want to clear the data, or click to remove the check mark if you want to keep the data.

10 Click the Clear button to remove all selected types of data. The process may take a few minutes to complete.

11 Click in the browser window outside the SETTINGS pane to close the pane. Leave Microsoft Edge open for the next skill.

Skill Extras

Clearing History and Data in Other Browsers

The table below shows how to clear your browser history and cookies in three popular browsers.

Browser	View History	Clear Browsing Data
Internet Explorer	Click the Favorites button (star) and then click the History tab in the pane that appears.	Click the Tools button (cog), point to *Safety* at the drop-down list, and then click *Delete browsing history*. At the Delete Browsing History dialog box, click the data type check boxes to insert or remove check marks, and then click Delete to remove all selected types of data.
Mozilla Firefox	Click the Open menu button (three horizontal stacked lines) and then click the History button.	Click the Open menu button (three horizontal stacked lines), click the History button, and then click *Clear Recent History*. At the dialog box, click the *Time range to clear* arrow, click the time range within which you want to clear browsing data (or click *Everything* to clear it all), and then click the Clear Now button.
Google Chrome	Click the Customize and control Google Chrome button (three horizontal stacked lines) and then click *History*.	Click the Customize and control Google Chrome button, click *History*, and then click the Clear browsing data button. In the Clear browsing data dialog box, click the data type check boxes to insert or remove check marks, and then click the Clear browsing data button to remove all selected types of data.

Blocking Cookies

A third-party cookie is one that is placed on your PC by an advertiser that doesn't directly have anything to do with the website you are visiting. You can choose to block third-party cookies in Microsoft Edge to prevent advertisers from tracking you (or at least make it more difficult for them to do so). In the SETTINGS pane, scroll down to the *Advanced settings* section, click the View advanced settings button, click the *Cookies* box arrow and then click *Block only third party cookies* at the drop-down list. You could click *Block all cookies*, but some websites might not work properly if you do so.

Skill 7

Print a Web Page

You can print a web page to create a hard copy of it that you can share offline with others. You can choose which printer to use, how many copies to print, and whether to print in portrait or landscape orientation. Depending on your chosen printer, you may also be able to adjust other settings.

Tutorial

2-3 *Another Way*
Press Ctrl + P.

TIP

Ask your instructor what printer to use if you are not sure.

TIP

Landscape orientation prints along the wide side of the paper; portrait prints along the narrow side. You can sometimes make a multipage print job fit on fewer sheets of paper by changing the orientation.

Online Extra

1 With Microsoft Edge open, click in the Address bar and then type http://W10.ParadigmCollege.net/Riley and press Enter, if that page is not already displayed from the previous skill.

2 Click the More actions button to open a menu.

3 Click *Print* to open the Print dialog box.

4 Click the *Printer* box arrow and then click the desired printer at the drop-down list, if it is not already selected.

5 Click the *Orientation* list box arrow and then click *Landscape* at the drop-down list.

6 Click the Print button if you want to print the page. Otherwise, click the Cancel button.

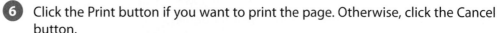

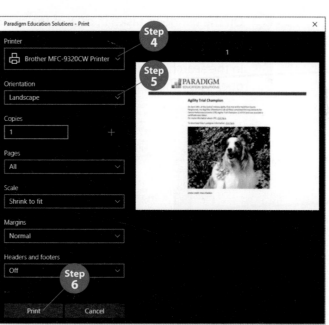

7 Close the Microsoft Edge browser window.

Skill Extra

Using More Print Settings

Before clicking Print in Step 6, you might want to click More settings to investigate the additional options available. These settings change depending on the printer you are using. For example, you might be able to change paper size, paper source, and collation options. (*Collation* refers to the order in which the pages print when you are printing multiple copies of a multipage file.)

Use Cortana to Get Information Online

Cortana is a personal assistant feature that has advanced search capabilities. It works on all Windows 10 devices, including tablets and phones. Cortana is woven tightly into almost every part of Window 10. You have already seen several examples of its usefulness:

- In Chapter 1, Skill 3, Cortana helped you find applications to run.
- In Chapter 1, Skill 7, Cortana served as a portal to Windows help information.
- In Chapter 2, Skill 9, Cortana helped you locate files and folders on your PC.

Cortana can also help you find information on the web. Cortana is able to process questions in natural language form, so you can phrase question as if you were talking to a real person. You aren't limited to simple keywords like in a regular web search.

When possible, Cortana answers within its own pane—no web browser is required. If you want to do more research on your own, or if Cortana can't answer the question you asked directly, you can click one of the links Cortana provides, such as a link to a Bing search.

Tutorial

TIP

If you press Enter in Step 2, you will go to whatever result is selected at the top of the results pane (probably the Bing search page), rather than allowing Cortana to find the answer.

TIP

To close the Cortana pane without opening Microsoft Edge, click away from the pane.

1. On the Windows taskbar, click in the search box. Cortana greets you with a pop-up pane.

2. Type What's the weather and then pause. Do not press Enter. Cortana will report the current temperature and conditions momentarily.

3. Click the current local temperature and conditions to open Microsoft Edge and display more weather details.

4. On the Windows taskbar, click in the search box, type tuna casserole recipe, and then pause. Again, do not press Enter.

5. In the search results list, click *tuna casserole recipe Search the web*. Microsoft Edge opens and shows search results for that topic.

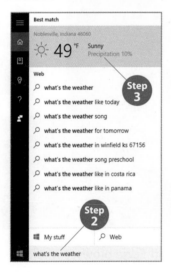

6. Close the Microsoft Edge browser window , clicking the Close all button when asked if you want to close all tabs.

Skill Extra

Using Voice Commands with Cortana

If your computer has a microphone, you can communicate with Cortana via voice commands. Just click the microphone symbol in the search box on the Windows taskbar to activate the voice feature and then speak clearly into your microphone. The first time you click the microphone symbol, Windows walks you through a brief setup process.

Task Summary

Task	Button/Icon/Option	Action
close browser tab	✕	In Microsoft Edge browser, click Close button on tab.
display Favorites list	☆	In Hub, click Favorites button.
download and open file from link	View downloads	On web page in Microsoft Edge browser, click link, click View downloads button. In Downloads list, click file.
duplicate browser tab	Duplicate tab	In Microsoft Edge browser, right-click tab, click *Duplicate tab*.
go back, go forward, or refresh web page	← → ↻	On Address bar in Microsoft Edge browser, click Back, Forward, or Refresh button.
go to a URL	http://paradigm.emcp.com	In Microsoft Edge browser, click in Address bar or search box, type address, press Enter.
open and close Hub	☰	On Address bar in Microsoft Edge browser, click Hub button to open Hub. Click away from Hub or press Esc to close it.
open and close Downloads list	↓	In Hub, click Downloads button to open list. Click outside list or press Esc to close it.
open new browser tab	+	In Microsoft Edge browser, click the New tab button.
print web page	Print	On web page in Microsoft Edge browser, click More actions button (…), click *Print*, choose settings, click Print button.
save and name favorite	☆	On web page in Microsoft Edge browser, click Add to favorites or reading list button (star), click Favorites button if needed, edit text in *Name* box, make sure *Favorites* appears in *Create in* list box, click Add button.
search web using Bing default search engine	🔍 Search or enter web address	In Microsoft Edge browser, click in Address bar or search box, type search term or phrase, press Enter, click search result.
search web using another search engine		In Microsoft Edge browser, navigate to search engine home page, type search term or phrase in search box, press Enter if needed, click search result.
start Microsoft Edge browser	e	On Windows taskbar, click Microsoft Edge button.
use Cortana to get information online	◯ Ask me anything 🎤	On Windows taskbar, click in search box, type search term or phrase and pause, click Cortana result or web search choice.
view browsing history	🕘	In Hub, click History button, click item to reopen it or click X on item to delete it.

Recheck

Workbook

Chapter study tools, exercises, and assessments are available in the Workbook, which is accessed through your ebook.

Chapter **4**

Precheck

Using OneDrive and Office Online Apps

In this chapter, you will learn how to use the web-based OneDrive interface to store, access, and manage files in OneDrive.

OneDrive is a Microsoft-provided cloud storage system. A *cloud storage system* is a secure online storage location that users can access from any computing device that has Internet access. Each Microsoft account has a certain amount of free storage space in OneDrive, and users can purchase additional space as needed. Many people use OneDrive to store personal files that they need to access from multiple devices. They can also share OneDrive files and folders with other online users.

Microsoft provides free web-based business productivity applications. These are simplified versions of the popular Microsoft Office applications, including Word, Excel, PowerPoint, Outlook, and OneNote. The Microsoft Online applications enable people to access Office data files even when using a computer that does not have the full desktop version of Microsoft Office installed. When you use these online apps, the default storage location is OneDrive.

Skills You Learn

1 Use File Explorer to Access OneDrive and Upload Student Data Files

2 Sign In to and Out of OneDrive.com

3 Navigate between Folders and Create a New Folder

4 Upload Files

5 Create a New Document in an Office Online App

6 Edit a File in an Office Online App

7 Share a Folder from OneDrive

 SNAP If you are a SNAP user, go to your SNAP Assignments page to complete the Precheck, Tutorials, and Recheck.

Files You Use

Before beginning this chapter, make sure you have copied the W10-StudentDataFiles folder to your USB flash drive. In the skills for this chapter, you will learn how to upload the entire folder to OneDrive and will use the data files listed here.

W10-C4-Birthdays.txt
W10-C4-Mortgage.xlsx

Skill 1

Use File Explorer to Access OneDrive and Upload Student Data Files

Each Microsoft account has its own separate OneDrive storage. When you sign in to Windows 10 with your Microsoft account, Windows automatically connects to the OneDrive server so you can access your OneDrive content via File Explorer. File Explorer includes a shortcut to OneDrive in the Navigation pane.

By default, Windows will *sync* OneDrive content to a folder on the local hard drive. In other words, Windows will keep a copy of everything from your OneDrive in a special user folder on your hard drive. This means that if the Internet is not available, you still have access to your content. This folder is stored in your user folders

(C: > Users > *username* > OneDrive).

When you work with OneDrive content on your local PC, you are technically working with local copies of content, not the online versions. However, the online versions are immediately synchronized to match the local versions whenever Internet access is available. You can therefore upload files and folders to OneDrive by placing them in your OneDrive folder in File Explorer. If your PC is not connected to the Internet, the synchronization automatically occurs whenever Internet connectivity becomes available.

Tutorial

You downloaded the student data files to a USB flash drive in Chapter 2, Skill 4.

4 *Another Way*
Click the *W10-StudentDataFiles* folder, click the Home tab, and then click the Copy button in the Clipboard group.
OR
Right-click the *W10-StudentDataFiles* folder and then click *Copy*.

1 Connect the USB flash drive containing the student data files for this textbook to your computer.

2 On the Windows taskbar, click the File Explorer button.

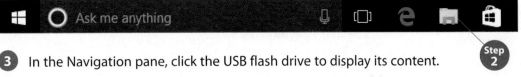

Step 2

3 In the Navigation pane, click the USB flash drive to display its content.

4 In the file list pane, click the *W10-StudentDataFiles* folder and then press Ctrl + C to copy it to the Clipboard.

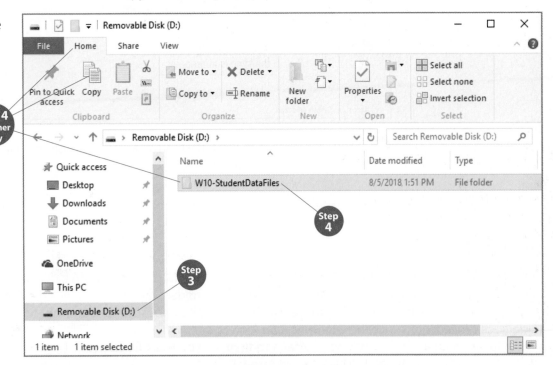

5 In the Navigation pane, click *OneDrive*. Your OneDrive files (if any) and folders appear in the file list pane.

TIP
The contents of your OneDrive account may not match the contents shown here.

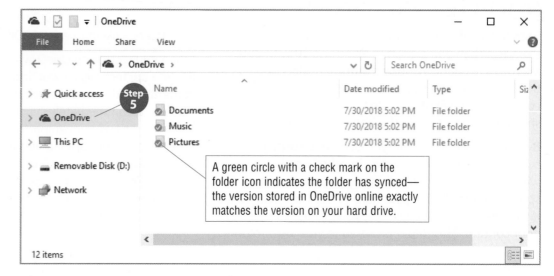

A green circle with a check mark on the folder icon indicates the folder has synced—the version stored in OneDrive online exactly matches the version on your hard drive.

6 *Another Way*
Right-click a blank area of the file list pane and then click *Paste*.
OR
Click the Home tab and then click the Paste button in the Clipboard group.

6 Press Ctrl + V to paste the copied folder into your OneDrive folder.

7 Click the Close button to close the File Explorer window.

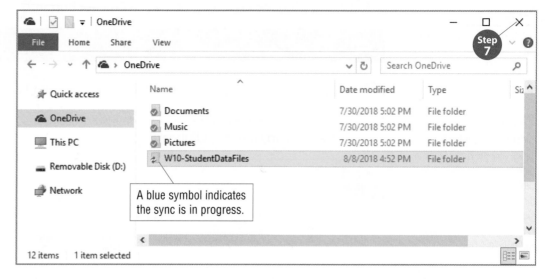

A blue symbol indicates the sync is in progress.

8 Safely disconnect the USB flash drive, as you learned to do in Chapter 2.

Skill Extra

Choosing Which Folders to Keep Synchronized

If you have a lot of content on your OneDrive, you might prefer not to sync all of it. To choose which folders are synced, right-click the OneDrive icon in the notification area of the Windows taskbar and then click *Settings*. (You might need to click the up arrow in the notification area to see the OneDrive icon.) At the Microsoft OneDrive dialog box, click the Choose folders tab and then click the Choose folders button. At the Choose what you want to sync screen, under *Sync only these folders*, click the check boxes to indicate how you want OneDrive to handle each folder. Click OK and then click OK again when you are finished.

Skill 2

Sign In to and Out of OneDrive.com

As you saw in Skill 1, you can work with OneDrive in a basic way through File Explorer. The online interface at OneDrive.com, however, provides even more capabilities. For example, using the online interface, you can share files with other users, and you can create new documents using Microsoft Office Online applications. The rest of this chapter assumes you are using the online version of OneDrive.

You can access OneDrive.com from any web browser. In this chapter you will use the Microsoft Edge browser, which is the default browser in Windows 10.

Tutorial

1 On the Windows taskbar, click the Microsoft Edge button to open the browser window.

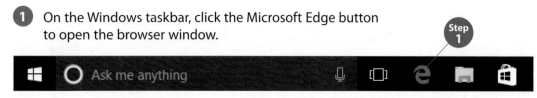

Step 1

2 *Another Way*
If MSN.com appears when you start Microsoft Edge, click the OneDrive icon near the top of the page.

2 Click in the search box, type onedrive.com, and then press Enter. If a *Files* section appears, you are already signed in, and you can skip to Step 8.

3 If you see an introductory page with Sign up and Sign in buttons in the upper right corner, click the Sign in button.

TIP
If you have previously signed out during this browser session, you might not see the prompts in Steps 3–5.

Step 3

4 Type the email address associated with your Microsoft account.

5 If there is a Next button, click Next.

Step 4

Step 5

6 In the *Password* text box, type your Microsoft account password.

7 Click the Sign in button.

8 Click the Account button in the upper right corner of the OneDrive.com page. A menu appears.

9 Click *Sign out*.

10 Close the Microsoft Edge browser window.

Skill Extras

Customizing the User Icon
By default, the Account button is a generic white profile image, as shown in the illustration for Step 8 of this skill. To change it to your own photo, click the Account button, click *Account settings* at the drop-down list, click *Add a photo* at your Microsoft account home page, and then follow the prompts to add a picture. The same picture will appear in all of your Microsoft applications.

Staying Signed In
If you are working with your own private computer, you might want to stay signed in to OneDrive.com. Click the *Keep me signed in* check box below the *Password* text box when you sign in, to insert a check mark. Windows will now remember you so you don't have to sign in each time you visit the website.

Skill 3

Navigate between Folders and Create a New Folder

After you sign in to OneDrive.com, you see folders in the file list pane on the right. If OneDrive opens in Thumbnail view, the folders appear as large tiles; if it opens in Details view, you see a list of small folders with names, dates modified, and other details. You might also see some files if you have previously used OneDrive with this Microsoft account.

As in File Explorer, the interface at OneDrive.com contains a Navigation pane on the left. The Navigation pane has the following links:

- *Files* is the OneDrive equivalent of *This PC* on your local PC. You can click *Files* at any time to come back to the top level of your OneDrive.
- *Recent* opens a list of data files that you have recently opened from OneDrive, if any, regardless of the folder they are in.

- *Photos* opens a list of photos stored on your OneDrive, regardless of the folder they are in.
- *Shared* opens a list of shortcuts to folders and files that either you have shared or someone else has shared with you.
- *Recycle bin* opens a list of files you have deleted from OneDrive.

You might also see a *PCs* link if your Microsoft account is set up on multiple computers.

The default folders include Documents, Music, and Pictures. (The Music folder might not appear until your Onedrive.com online storage is synchronized with your Windows 10 PC.) You can use the default folders, create your own folders, or copy folders from your local PC to OneDrive. In this skill, you learn to create a folder and name it.

Tutorial

TIP

You copied the folder W10-StudentDataFiles to OneDrive in Skill 1. If it does not appear immediately in Step 1, wait a few minutes for your PC and OneDrive.com to sync.

TIP

At OneDrive.com, clicking an item opens it; in File Explorer, clicking an item selects it and double-clicking opens it.

1 Open Microsoft Edge, go to OneDrive.com, and sign in to your account, as you learned in Skill 2.

2 With *Files* selected in the Navigation pane, click the *W10-StudentDataFiles* thumbnail in the file list pane to open the folder.

If the Navigation pane doesn't display, widen the browser window.

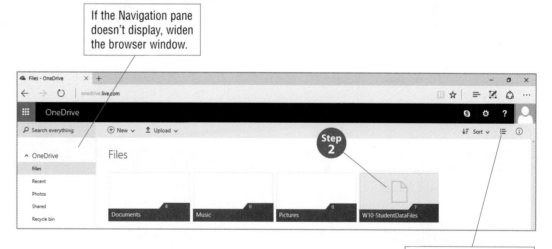

Click the View button if the folders do not display as shown here in Step 2.

In Details view, clicking or double-clicking the name of an item opens the item, and clicking the date modified, sharing indicator, or size selects the item.

4 *Another Way*
Click *Files* in the Navigation pane to return to the top level of the OneDrive folder structure.

5 *Another Way*
Right-click a blank area of the file list pane and then click *Create*.

3 In the upper right corner of the file list pane, click the View button. Notice that the display changes to show the folders in Details view.

4 Click the Back button in the browser window to return to the previous location.

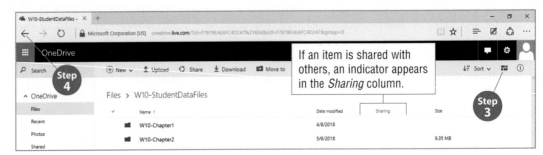

If an item is shared with others, an indicator appears in the *Sharing* column.

5 On the bar at the top of the page, click the New button.

6 Click *Folder* at the drop-down list.

7 At the Folder dialog box, type W10-C4-Miscellaneous in the *Folder name* box.

8 Click the Create button. The new folder appears in the file list pane. Leave Microsoft Edge open at OneDrive.com for the next skill.

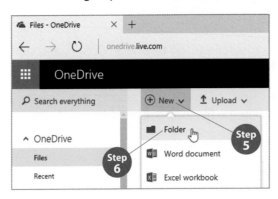

Skill Extra

Using Other File-Handling Skills

All the same file and folder management skills you learned in Chapter 2 can also be accomplished at OneDrive.com. Here's a quick overview of file-handling skills in OneDrive.
Hint: If you don't see a certain button on the bar across the top of the OneDrive page, click the More (...) button to see undisplayed commands, or widen your browser window.

Skill	Method	Alternative Method
Select a file or folder	In Details view, point to the left of the file name, click round check circle that appears.	In Thumbnails view, point to upper right corner of tile, click check circle that appears.
Rename a file or folder	Select item, click Rename button on bar at top of page, type new name, press Enter.	Right-click item, click *Rename*, type new name, press Enter.
Delete a file or folder	Select item, click Delete button on bar at top of page.	Right-click item, click *Delete*.
Move a file or folder	Select item, click Move to button on bar at top of page, select destination, click Move button.	Right-click item, click *Move to*, select destination, click Move button.
Copy a file	Select item, click Copy to button on bar at top of page, select destination, click Copy button.	Right-click item, click *Copy to*, select destination, click Copy button.

Skill 4

Upload Files

Copying files from your local PC to an online storage location such as OneDrive is called *uploading*. Uploading is the opposite of *downloading*, which means copying an item from an online storage location to your local PC. Note that uploading and downloading make copies of files; they do not move the original files.

You might upload a file so that it will be available when you use a different computer, or in preparation for sharing the file online with others (covered in Skill 7).

Uploading via OneDrive.com has the same end result as uploading via File Explorer (covered in Skill 1). The OneDrive.com method works directly with the online storage location, however, whereas File Explorer interacts with the copy on your hard drive. As a result, uploads performed via OneDrive.com are immediate, whereas uploads performed with File Explorer may take a few minutes to synchronize.

Tutorial

1 Connect the USB flash drive containing the student data files for this textbook to your computer.

2 With Microsoft Edge open to the file list pane in your OneDrive.com account, click the Upload button.

3 In the Navigation pane of the Open dialog box, click the USB flash drive where your downloaded student data files are stored, navigate to the W10-Chapter4 folder on your flash drive, and then click **W10-C4-Birthdays** to select it.

4 Press and hold the Shift key as you click **W10-C4-Mortgage** to select it also.

5 Click the Open button. Wait for the files to finish uploading and appear in the file list pane.

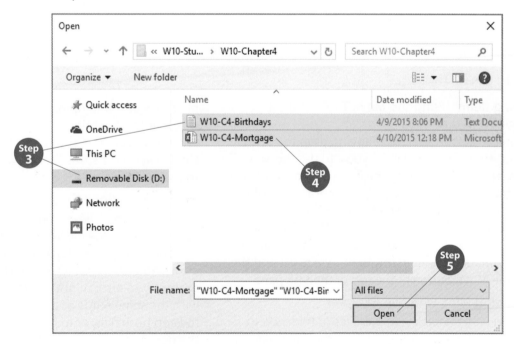

6 In the file list pane, point to the left of each file you just uploaded, and then click in the check circles that appear to insert check marks and select the files.

7 Drag the selected files and drop them on the W10-C4-Miscellaneous folder, moving them there. Leave Microsoft Edge open to your file list pane at OneDrive.com for the next skill.

TIP

If your file list pane does not match the one shown here, you are not in Details view. Click the View button in the upper right corner of the page to switch to Details view if needed.

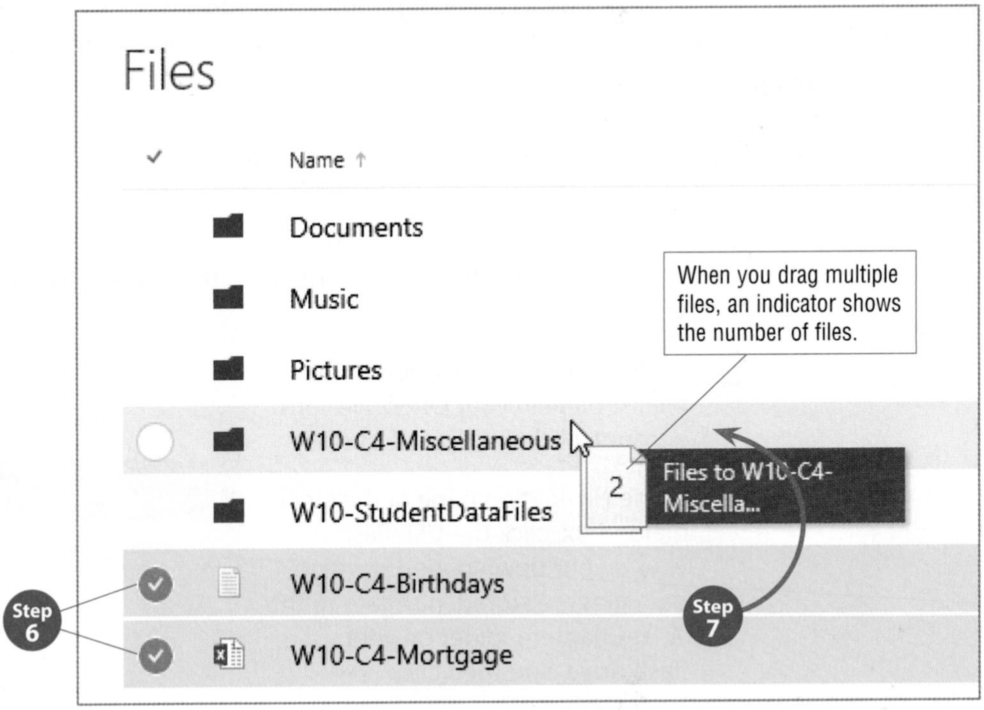

Skill Extras

Moving Items Using the Move To Command in OneDrive

At OneDrive.com, you can drag and drop to move files (as shown in this skill) or you can use the Move To command. After selecting the files you want to move, click the Move To button on the bar at the top of the page. (If you do not see the Move To button, click the Other button [...] and then click the *Move To* option in the drop-down list.) In the task pane that opens, click the destination folder in the *Move item to* list and then click the Move button at the top of the task pane.

Uploading Files with File Explorer

Another way to quickly upload files or folders is to use File Explorer to copy them into the OneDrive folder in your user folders on your PC. You learned

how to access and upload to this folder in Skill 1 of this chapter. Anything you place in the OneDrive user folder on your PC is automatically uploaded to your OneDrive online storage area while you are connected to the Internet.

Resolving Upload Errors

After you upload files to OneDrive, an Error icon ( ) appears above the file list if one or more files did not upload correctly. Click this icon to see a list of errors, and then click an action to resolve an error. For example, an error might occur if you try to upload a file with the same name as an existing file. You can choose to keep both files, or to replace the existing file with the new one.

Create a New Document in an Office Online App

From OneDrive.com, you can access several Microsoft Office Online applications. These are simplified versions of the corresponding desktop applications, including Word, Excel, PowerPoint, and OneNote. These applications offer a convenient way of creating and editing Office-compatible content even if you are using a computer that does not have the full desktop version of Microsoft Office installed. When you create a new file using one of the online Office apps, OneDrive saves your work automatically. The steps provided here use Word as an example, but they also work in most of the other Office Online apps too.

Tutorial

TIP

When creating a new file, start by selecting the location to store it—in this case, the top folder level of your OneDrive.

1 With Microsoft Edge open to the file list pane in your OneDrive.com account, click *Files* in the Navigation pane to ensure you are starting at the top folder level.

2 On the bar at the top of the page, click the New button.

3 Click *Word document* at the drop-down list.

4 In the new Word Online document that opens, type your full name and then press Enter.

5 Type your school name and then drag across the school name to select it.

TIP

The HOME tab contains commands for formatting text, including character formatting like bold, italic, and underline.

6 Click the HOME tab on the ribbon and then click the Bold button in the Font group.

7 On the bar at the top of the page, click the name of the file you are working in. It will be a generic name, such as *Document1*.

8 Type W10-C4-School and then press Enter to rename the file.

9 On the bar at the top of the page, click OneDrive to return to the OneDrive file list.

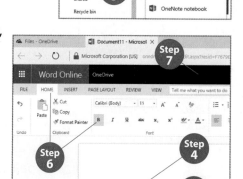

Online Extra

10 In the file list pane, drag the **W10-C4-School** file to the W10-C4-Miscellaneous folder and drop it there. The file moves to that folder. Leave Microsoft Edge open to your file list pane at OneDrive.com for the next skill.

Skill Extra

Printing Your Work

With the Online apps, you can't print directly to a printer on your local PC. When you issue the Print command (click the FILE tab, click the *Print* option, and then click the Print button), the application creates a PDF. Click *Click here to view the PDF of your Document* to display the PDF in a new browser tab. You can then print the PDF using your browser's Print feature.

Edit a File in an Office Online App

At OneDrive.com, it is easy to open and edit a data file that is supported by a Microsoft Office Online app. Simply click the file, and it opens in the appropriate app. For example, if you click a Word document, it opens in Word Online. If you click a file that is not supported by an Office Online app, OneDrive downloads it to your local hard drive and then offers you an Open button. This allows you to try to open the file using the applications installed on your PC.

Tutorial

TIP

You created the folder W10-C4-Miscellaneous in Skill 3 and added files to it in Skills 4 and 5.

1 With Microsoft Edge open to the file list pane in your OneDrive.com account, click *Files* in the Navigation pane to ensure you are starting at the top folder level.

2 Click the W10-C4-Miscellaneous folder link to view the folder's content.

3 Click the **W10-C4-Mortgage** file link to open the file in Excel Online.

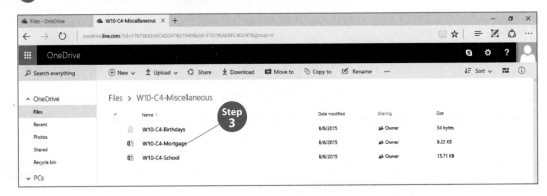

TIP

If the ribbon does not appear and you are not able to edit the file in Step 4, see the Skill Extra following these steps.

TIP

In Step 5, the amount in cell B6 also changes because the cell contains a formula that links to cell B3. See Excel Help for information about formulas.

TIP

Your changes are saved automatically when you close a tab displaying an Office Online file.

4 Click cell B3 (at the intersection of column B and row 3) to make it active.

5 Type $350,000 and then press Enter. Notice that the amount in cell B3 changes to the new value.

6 On the W10-C4-Mortgage.xlsx tab in the browser window, click the Close button. Leave Microsoft Edge open to your file list pane at OneDrive.com for the next skill.

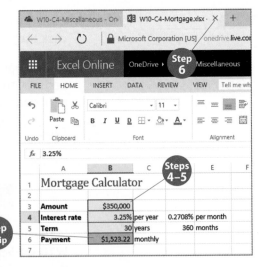

Online Extras

Skill Extra

Switching between Reading View and Editing View
If a file opens in Reading view, the ribbon doesn't appear and you can't edit the file. Click the edit button (Edit Document for Word, Edit Workbook for Excel, and so on) to open a menu, and then click the option for editing in the desktop application or online (for example, *Edit in Excel Online*). To change back to Reading mode, click the VIEW tab and then click the Reading View button in the Document Views group.

Share a Folder from OneDrive

You can share your OneDrive content with other people, whether they are in the same office or halfway around the world. You can allow others to edit the files, or you can make the sharing read-only. If someone has the link to the folder, they can access it by that link in any web browser. Users with read-only access to a shared file or folder may download it and make changes to their own copy.

You can share individual files or entire folders. Sharing a folder simplifies the process of sharing multiple files because anything you later place inside that folder will be shared with the same permissions as the folder itself.

Tutorial

2 *Another Way*
Click the W10-C4-Miscellaneous folder to select it and then click the Share button on the bar above the file listing.

TIP

Right-click an individual file instead of a folder if you want to share only one file.

1 With Microsoft Edge open to the file list pane in your OneDrive.com account, click *Files* in the Navigation pane to ensure you are starting at the top folder level.

2 Right-click the <u>W10-C4-Miscellaneous</u> folder link and then click *Share* at the shortcut menu.

3 Click *Get a link* in the left pane of the Share dialog box.

4 Click the *Choose an option* box arrow and then click *Edit* at the drop-down list, if needed.

5 Click the Create link button.

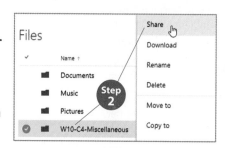

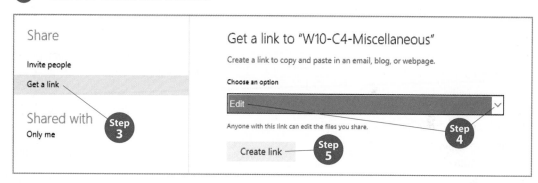

6 Click the *Shorten link* option.

7 Click in the *Edit* text box to select the link, and then press Ctrl + C to copy the link to the Clipboard. From the Clipboard, you could paste this link anywhere, such as in an email or a social media post.

TIP

Shortening the link in Step 6 creates a shorter alias address, which may be easier to share with others. Shortening a link is optional.

8 Click the Close button in the Share dialog box.

9 In the Navigation pane, click *Shared*. Notice that the W10-C4-Miscellaneous folder appears under the *Shared by me* heading in the file list pane.

Online Extra

10 Sign out of OneDrive.com and then close the browser window.

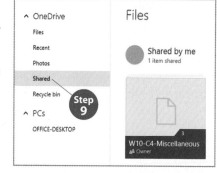

Skill Extra

Finding a Link Address Again

Any time you need to get the link for a shared folder, you can easily retrieve it. Right-click the shared folder in the file list pane and then click *Share* at the shortcut menu. Click the icon under the *Shared with* heading to display the link address.

Task Summary

Task	Button/Icon/Option	Action
access OneDrive using File Explorer	﹥ ☁ OneDrive	In Navigation pane of File Explorer window, click *OneDrive*.
change to Details view or Thumbnails view at OneDrive.com	☰ ▦	On bar at top of page, click View button.
close Office Online file at OneDrive.com	✕	On file tab at top of page, click Close button.
copy selected file or folder at OneDrive.com	📋 Copy to	On bar at top of page, click Copy to button, select destination, click Copy button.
copy selected files or folders into OneDrive using File Explorer	Copy Paste	In File Explorer window, copy desired item(s), click *OneDrive* in Navigation pane, open desired OneDrive folder in file list pane, paste item(s) into folder.
create and name new Office Online document at OneDrive.com	⊕ New ⌄	On bar at top of page, click New button, click file type at drop-down list.
create and name new folder at OneDrive.com	📁 Folder	Navigate to desired folder location, click New button on bar at top of page, click *Folder*, type name, click Create button.
delete file or folder at OneDrive.com	🗑 Delete	In file list pane, select item, click Delete button on bar at top of page.
edit file in Office Online app at OneDrive.com	📄 W10-C4-Mortgage	In file list pane, click file, switch to Editing view if necessary to display ribbon.
move file or folder at OneDrive.com	➡ Move to	In file list pane, select item, click Move to button on bar at top of page, select destination, click Move button.
move files using drag-and-drop at OneDrive.com		In file list pane, select files, drag files, drop files on destination.
navigate to folder at OneDrive.com	Files	In Navigation pane, click *Files*, click desired folder.
rename file or folder at OneDrive.com	✎ Rename	In file list pane, select item, click Other things (...) button on bar at top of page, click *Rename*, type new name, press Enter.
return to OneDrive from Office Online app	OneDrive	In Office Online document tab in browser, click *OneDrive* on bar at top of page.
select file or folder at OneDrive.com	◯	In Details view, point to left of file name, click check circle. In Thumbnails view, point to upper right corner of tile, click check circle.
share file or folder at OneDrive.com	⟳ Share	In file list pane, right-click file or folder, click *Share*, click *Get a link*, click *Choose an option* box arrow, click *Edit*, click Create link button, copy link, click Close button, paste link where desired.
sign in to OneDrive.com		At introductory page, click Sign in button, type Microsoft account email address, click Next, type password, click Sign in button.
sign out of OneDrive.com	Sign out	On bar at top of page, click user profile image, click *Sign out*.
upload files at OneDrive.com	⬆ Upload	On bar at top of page, click Upload, navigate to files, select files, click Open button.

Recheck

Workbook

Chapter study tools, exercises, and assessments are available in the Workbook, which is accessed through your ebook.

Chapter 5

Precheck

Taking Screenshots and Using OneNote

In this chapter, you will learn how to create a graphic file of what you see on your computer screen and send that file to others via email. This type of graphic is commonly called a *screenshot* or *screen capture*. You might need to create and email screenshots for a computer applications class. For example, your instructor might ask you to take a screenshot to show you have completed a certain exercise. You might also find it useful to take screenshots for your own reference or to share with a friend. There are several ways to create these, including using the Print Screen key to take Windows screen captures and using the Snipping tool in Windows.

This chapter also covers the Office Online version of *Microsoft OneNote*, an Office application that stores and organizes content from many different sources in one easy-to-access place. You might use OneNote to organize the research you gather for a report or to share your research findings with a group of classmates or coworkers.

Skills You Learn

1 Capture an Image of the Entire Screen

2 Use the Snipping Tool to Capture a Portion of the Screen

3 Email an Image Using the Snipping Tool

4 Create a Notebook, Sections, and Pages in OneNote

5 Add Content to a Page in OneNote

6 Collect and Organize Online Content in OneNote

7 Email a Link to OneNote Content

 **SNAP**   If you are a SNAP user, go to your SNAP Assignments page to complete the Precheck, Tutorials, and Recheck.

Files You Use

Before beginning this chapter, make sure you have copied the W10-StudentDataFiles folder to your USB flash drive. For the skills in this chapter, you will use the data file listed in the next column.

W10-C5-Duncan.png

Capture an Image of the Entire Screen

The most basic way to take a screenshot is to press the Print Screen key on your keyboard. (Depending on your keyboard, you may need to press a combination of keys such as Fn + PrntScn or Shift + PrntScr.) This command copies an image of the entire screen to the Windows Clipboard, which you learned about in Chapter 2. You can then paste the image into some other application. For example, you can paste it into a graphics program like Paint, or a word processing program like Word or WordPad.

If you want to save the captured image as a graphic file without having to paste it into a particular program, you can press the Windows logo key as you press the Print Screen key. This will capture the entire screen, place a copy on the Clipboard, and also save the graphic as a PNG file in a Screenshots folder within your Pictures folder.

Tutorial

① Another Way
Click the Start button and then click *File Explorer* at the Start menu.

TIP

Pressing Windows + Print Screen in Step 2 saves the screenshot on the Clipboard and also as a PNG file on your computer.

TIP

If you don't see *Pictures* in Step 3, click *This PC* in the Navigation pane.

**① ** On the Windows taskbar, click the File Explorer button.

**② ** Press the Windows logo key () and hold it down while you press and then release the Print Screen key. The screen dims briefly and then returns to normal.

**③ ** In the file list pane, double-click the *Pictures* folder to open it.

TIP

Captured screenshot files are named *Screenshot* with a number in parentheses, such as *Screenshot (1)*.

Online Extra

**④ ** Double-click the *Screenshots* folder to open it. Notice that your captured screenshot file is stored here.

Skill Extra

Saving Screen Captures in a Different File Format
If you want to save a screenshot in a format other than PNG, press Print Screen to capture the screen. (Pressing Print Screen by itself saves the screenshot only on the Clipboard, not on your computer.) Open the Paint application, paste the image into the Paint window, click the File tab, click *Save As*, and then click the *Save as type* drop-down list box arrow to choose a different file type. The choices available include *Bitmap (.bmp)*, *JPEG (.jpg)*, *GIF (.gif)*, *TIFF (.tif)*, and *PNG (.png)*. Other graphics applications such as Photoshop and Paint Shop Pro offer even more file format choices.

5–6 *Another Way*
Click the microphone icon on the search box and then say, "Start wordpad," into the PC's microphone.

TIP

If you have never used the microphone in Windows 10 before, you are prompted to complete a short setup process the first time you click the microphone icon.

5 Click in the search box on the Windows taskbar and then type wordpad.

6 In the search results, click *WordPad Desktop app* to open a new, blank document.

Your captured screenshot is stored in the Screenshots folder by default.

7 *Another Way*
Press Ctrl + V.

7 On the Home tab in the WordPad window, click the Paste button in the Clipboard group. Your screenshot is pasted from the Clipboard into the WordPad document.

8 Click the Close button to close the WordPad window.

9 When prompted to save changes, click the Don't Save button. Leave File Explorer open for the next skill.

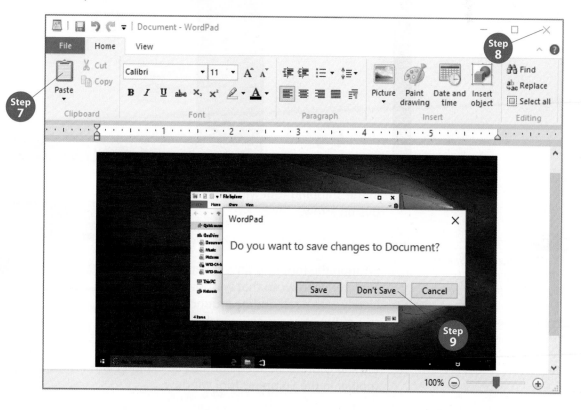

Skill 2
Use the Snipping Tool to Capture a Portion of the Screen

Sometimes you might want to capture only part of a screen—such as a single dialog box or one corner of an open window. One way to achieve that result is to capture the entire screen, open the captured screenshot in a picture editing program such as Paint, and then crop the image. However, there is an easier way: use the Snipping Tool.

Snipping Tool is a Windows application. You can use it to capture a part of the screen, copy the image to the Clipboard, and then paste the image anywhere you like. You can also save the image as a file or send it in an email as part of the message body or as an attachment.

Tutorial

1 With File Explorer open, connect the USB flash drive containing the W10-StudentDataFiles folder to your PC.

2 On the Windows taskbar, type snip in the search box.

3 In the search results, click *Snipping Tool Desktop app* to open the Snipping Tool application.

4 In the Snipping Tool window, click the New button arrow.

5 At the drop-down list, click *Window Snip*.

TIP

The New button drop-down list offers four options: *Free-form Snip* (define a free-form area), *Rectangular Snip* (define a rectangular area), *Window Snip* (select a specific window), and *Full-screen Snip* (capture the full screen).

6 Position the mouse pointer over the File Explorer window so that window is shown clearly with a red outline around it and the rest of the screen is covered with a frosted haze.

7 Click to capture an image of the File Explorer window and display it below the toolbar in the Snipping Tool window.

8 On the Snipping Tool toolbar, click the Copy button to copy the image to the Windows Clipboard.

9 Click the Save Snip button to open the Save As dialog box.

TIP

The W10-Chapter5 folder is located in your W10-StudentDataFiles folder.

10 At the dialog box, navigate to the W10-Chapter5 folder on your USB flash drive.

11 In the *File name* text box, type W10-C5-S2-Snip to replace the default file name.

12 Click the Save button to save the snip as a new file. Leave the Snipping Tool window open and your USB flash drive connected for the next skill.

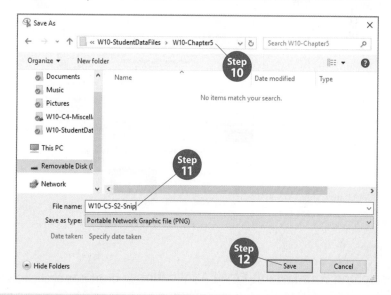

Skill Extra

Annotating Snips

After you capture a snip, you can use the Pen tool on the Snipping Tool toolbar to write on the image by dragging the mouse pointer (or your finger, if you have a touchscreen) over the image; for example, you could circle the most important area of the image. Beside the Pen tool is the Highlighter tool, which works like a

real highlighter; drag across an area to highlight it. The Eraser tool erases your pen and highlighter marks.

Skill 3

Email an Image Using the Snipping Tool

After capturing a snip, you can use the Snipping Tool to email it to someone via your default email application. If Microsoft Office is installed on your PC, the default is probably Microsoft Outlook, which is used in this skill. If you do not have a default email application set up on your PC or are not sure whether you do, see the instructions in the Skill Extra before beginning the skill steps.

Tutorial

TIP

If the Snipping Tool is not still open when you start this skill, repeat Steps 1–8 of Skill 2.

TIP

In Step 2, if you see a message that there is no email program associated, click OK and then follow the instructions in the Skill Extra.

TIP

If this is the first time you have used your default email application, you might be prompted to go through a setup process. After it completes, you may have to restart these steps.

TIP

To confirm your email was sent, open your email application and check the Sent Items folder.

Online Extra

1 Start with the Snipping Tool window open and the snip you captured in Skill 2 displayed below the toolbar, and your USB flash drive connected.

2 On the Snipping Tool toolbar, click the Send Snip button to open a new email window in your default email application, with the snipped image appearing in the body of the email message.

3 In the *To* box, type the recipient's email address. ***Note:*** *Ask your instructor what email address to use.*

4 In the *Subject* box, select the text that appears there by default and then type Chapter 5 Skill 3 to replace it.

5 Click the Send button. The email application sends the message and then closes.

6 Close all open windows and safely disconnect your USB flash drive.

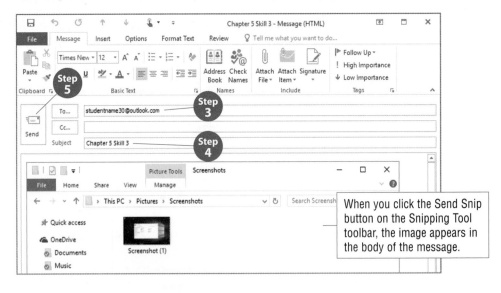

When you click the Send Snip button on the Snipping Tool toolbar, the image appears in the body of the message.

Skill Extra

Changing or Setting Your Default Email Application

To complete this skill, a desktop app such as Outlook must be your default email app. If your default email app is a Modern app, such as Mail, you must change the default.

To change or set your default email application in Windows 10, click in the search box on the Windows taskbar and then type default. In the search results list, click *Choose a default email app*. Under *Email* in the right pane, click the current default email application (or click *Choose a default* if that is your only option) and then click the desired application at the menu. If the only menu option is *Look for an app in the Store*, you do not have any eligible email applications and will need to install one. Note that a web-based email interface such as Outlook.com, Gmail, or Yahoo! mail cannot be set as a default application.

Skill 4
Create a Notebook, Sections, and Pages in OneNote

OneNote is an application for organizing notes and data, such as research for a school paper or a work project. You can include website content, documents, pictures, and more. The most basic organizing unit of OneNote is a *notebook*. Within a notebook, you can have *sections*, which are like dividers. Each section can have one or more *pages*. In this skill, you will create a notebook, two sections, and two pages.

There are two versions of OneNote: the desktop version that comes with Microsoft Office 2016, and the free online version that is part of the Office Online suite. In this chapter, you will work with OneNote Online.

Tutorial

TIP

You learned about Microsoft Edge in Chapter 3. You learned how to sign in to OneDrive in Chapter 4.

1 Open Microsoft Edge, go to OneDrive.com, and sign in to your account if prompted.

2 At the Navigation pane, click *Files* to ensure you are at the top level of your OneDrive storage.

3 On the bar at the top of the page, click the New button and then click *OneNote notebook*.

4 At the OneNote notebook dialog box, type W10-C5-Notebook in the text box.

5 Click the Create button to open your new notebook at a new, blank page in OneNote.

6 At the insertion point in the title area of the page, type Page 1 and press Enter.

7 Right-click *Untitled Section* in the Navigation pane and then click *Rename*.

8 At the Section Name dialog box, type Content in the *Enter a section name* box.

9 Click the OK button.

10 On the ribbon, click the INSERT tab and then click the New Page button in the Notebook group to create a new page.

11 At the insertion point in the title area of the new page, type Page 2.

12 On the ribbon, click the INSERT tab and then click the New Section button in the Notebook group to create a new section.

13 At the Section Name dialog box, type Miscellaneous in the *Enter a section name* box.

14 Click OK. Leave OneNote open for the next skill.

TIP

If you don't see the Navigation pane in Step 6, click the Navigation pane button (with three horizontal lines) to the left of the page title and then click the Pin Pane icon to make the pane stay open.

10 Another Way
In the Navigation pane, click + *Page*.

12 Another Way
In the Navigation pane, click + *Section*.

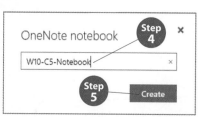

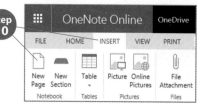

Skill Extra

Working with Other Notebooks

You can create a new notebook at any time by returning to the OneDrive tab in your browser window and repeating Steps 2–5 of this skill to assign a different name to the notebook. To open an existing notebook, select it from the file listing in OneDrive.

Add Content to a Page in OneNote

Within a OneNote page, you can type text directly, like in a word processing program. You can also format text using the same basic character and paragraph formatting tools available in Microsoft Word, including tools for applying different styles, bulleted and numbered lists, fonts, font sizes, and font colors. You can also insert pictures on a notebook page. In this skill, you will see how to place both text and a picture on a notebook page.

Tutorial

You created the notebook W10-C5-Notebook in Skill 4.

1 With the W10-C5-Notebook notebook open in OneNote Online, connect the USB flash drive containing your W10-StudentDataFiles folder to your PC.

2 In the Navigation pane, click the *Content* section and then click the *Page 1* page.

3 In the right pane, click to move the insertion point below the page title and then type This is a picture of Duncan at the dog show. Press Enter twice.

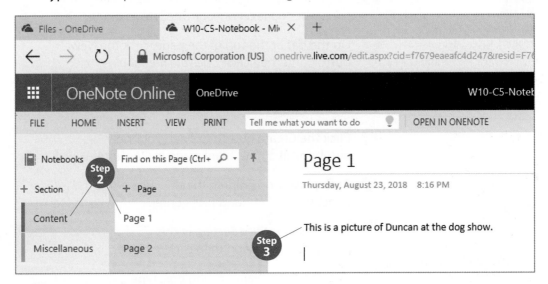

4 On the ribbon, click the INSERT tab and then click the Picture button in the Pictures group.

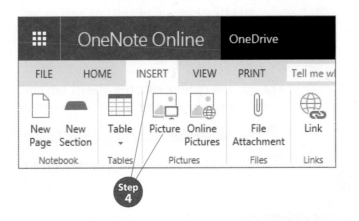

5 At the Open dialog box, navigate to the W10-Chapter5 folder on your USB flash drive.

6 Click the **W10-C5-Duncan** file to select it.

7 Click the Open button to insert the picture on the notebook page at the insertion point position.

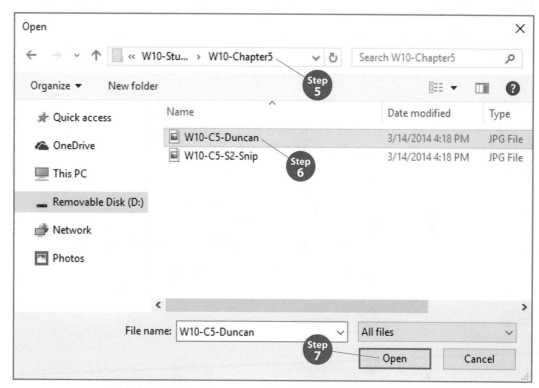

8 Right-click the picture in the notebook page and then click *Shrink* at the shortcut menu. The picture shrinks in size.

9 Click twice in the text above the picture to deselect the picture. Leave OneNote Online open to this page for the next skill. Safely disconnect your USB flash drive.

Skill Extras

Printing a OneNote Online Notebook Page

To print a OneNote Online notebook page, start by clicking the PRINT tab on the ribbon. At the Print dialog box, use options to specify settings such as the desired printer, number of copies, orientation (portrait or landscape), and color mode. (The options will vary depending on the printer or printers available to your PC.) After making all your selections, click the Print button.

Tagging Content in OneNote Online

On the HOME tab of the OneNote ribbon, the Tag button in the Tags group opens a menu of tags, which are like categories. You can tag a piece of content to assign a category to it, such as Question, Definition, or Idea.

Skill 6

Collect and Organize Online Content in OneNote

OneNote Online works with the Windows Clipboard, which means that you can paste almost any type of content into a notebook page. For example, you can copy and paste text, images, and links from other Windows applications, websites, and email messages.

You can use OneNote to organize lists of web addresses. This can be helpful when gathering sources for a school research paper or a workplace project. Saving web addresses in OneNote has advantages over simply bookmarking them in your web browser. It allows you to access them no matter which browser you are using, and to group and categorize the links for easier retrieval. You can also choose to make text notes about each link to help you remember why you saved it.

Tutorial

Insert a Picture from a Web Page in a OneNote Page

1 Make sure the W10-C5-Notebook notebook is open in OneNote.

2 In your browser, open a new tab and then navigate to the location http://W10.ParadigmCollege.net/Riley.

3 Right-click the photo on the web page and then click *Copy picture* at the shortcut menu.

4 Switch back to the OneNote tab in your browser.

5 Display the Navigation pane if needed, and then click *Page 1* to switch to that page if necessary.

6 Scroll down to the bottom of Page 1 and click to place the insertion point below the existing picture. Press Enter.

7 Type Here is Riley with his blue ribbon. Press Enter twice.

8 Press Ctrl + V to paste the new picture in this location.

9 Right-click the pasted picture and then click *Shrink* at the shortcut menu. Click *Shrink* two more times to shrink the picture even further.

Insert a Link in a OneNote Page

Tutorial

10 Navigate to Page 2 in your notebook.

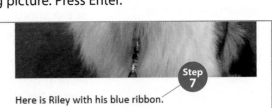

Here is Riley with his blue ribbon.
Step 7

Step 9 — Grow / Shrink / Cut / Copy / Paste

TIP

To switch browser tabs in Step 4, click the desired tab at the top of the Microsoft Edge window. See Chapter 3 for more information about using Microsoft Edge.

TIP

In Step 8, if a message appears asking if you want to allow this web page to access your Clipboard, click Allow access.

TIP

If needed, display the Navigation pane and then click *Page 2*.

⑪ Click to move the insertion point below the page title in the right pane and then type Here's the announcement of Margaret's dog winning his C-ATCH title: http://W10.ParadigmCollege.net/Riley. **Press Enter twice.**

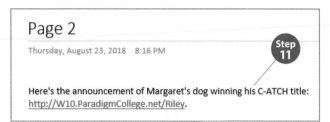

⑫ On the ribbon, click the INSERT tab and then click the Link button in the Links group.

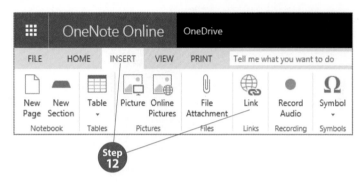

⑬ At the Link dialog box, click in the *Display text* box and then type CPE Home Page.

⑭ Click in the *Address* box, and then type http://W10.ParadigmCollege.net/CPE.

⑮ Click Insert. The hyperlink appears on the notebook page with the text you specified: CPE Home Page.

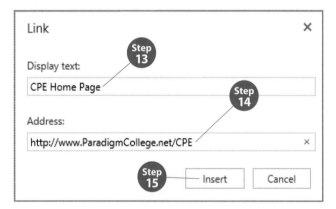

⑯ Leave OneNote Online open at this page for the next skill.

Skill Extra

Copying and Pasting Web Addresses

Here's a shortcut method for capturing a web page's address in OneNote: Display the desired web page in your web browser, select its address in the Address bar, and then press Ctrl + C to copy the address. In your OneNote notebook page, position the insertion point where you want the address to appear and then press Ctrl + V to paste the link at that location.

Skill 7

Email a Link to OneNote Content

It is easy to share your OneNote content with other people. You can send an email containing a link to your OneNote file on your OneDrive, and others can use OneNote Online to view the notebook. For example, you could place your assignments in a OneNote notebook and then invite your instructor to view it for grading. You can share a OneNote notebook by creating a link to it and sharing the link, as you did in Chapter 4, or you can send an email directly from OneNote.

Tutorial

1. Start with your W10-C5-Notebook file open in OneNote Online.

2. On the ribbon, click the FILE tab.

3. Click *Share* and then click *Share with People*.

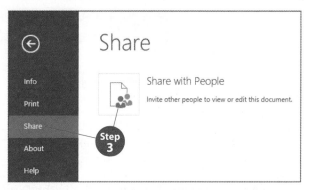

TIP

Ask your instructor what email address to use for the recipient in Step 4.

4. In the *To* box, type the email address to which you want to send an invitation.

5. In the *Add a quick note* box, type Here is a link to my W10-C5-Notebook file in OneNote.

6. Click Share.

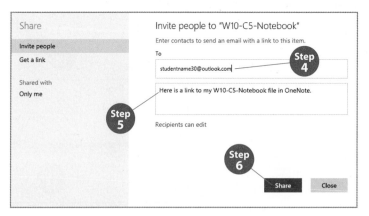

7. Click Close.

8. Close the Microsoft Edge browser window.

Skill Extra

Restricting Others from Editing Your Notebook
If you don't want the recipient to be able to edit your notebook, click *Recipients can edit* between Steps 3 and 4. Click the *Recipients can edit* box arrow and then click *Recipients can only view* at the drop-down list.

Task Summary

Task	Button/Icon/Option	Action
capture a portion of the screen with Snipping Tool	● Window Snip	On toolbar, click New button arrow, click *Window Snip*, click New button, point to window, click window.
create and name OneNote notebook in OneDrive	OneNote notebook	On bar at top of OneDrive page, click New button, click *OneNote notebook*, type name, click Create button.
create and name notebook page in OneNote Online	New Page	On ribbon, click INSERT tab, click New Page button in Notebook group, type page title.
create and name notebook section in OneNote Online	New Section	On ribbon, click INSERT tab, click New Section button in Notebook group, type name, click OK.
email image from Snipping Tool		On toolbar, click Send Snip button. In email window, fill in *To* and *Subject* boxes, click Send button.
email content from OneNote Online	Share	On ribbon, click FILE tab, click *Share*, click *Share with People*. In *To* box, type email address, click Share button, click Close button.
enter text in notebook page in OneNote Online		Click in desired location below title, type text.
insert online content link in notebook page in OneNote Online	Link	Click desired position. On ribbon, click INSERT tab, click Link button in Links group. In *Display text* box, type link text. In *Address* box, type web page address. Click Insert button.
insert picture in notebook page in OneNote Online	Picture	Click desired position. On ribbon, click INSERT tab, click Picture button in Pictures group. In Open dialog box, navigate to folder, click picture file, click Open button.
navigate to a page in OneNote Online		In Navigation pane, click desired section, click desired page.
save and name screenshot in Snipping Tool		On toolbar, click Save Snip button. In Save As dialog box, navigate to folder, type name in *File name* text box, click Save button.
start Snipping Tool	Snipping Tool Desktop app	On Windows taskbar, type snip in search box, click *Snipping Tool*.
type online content link in notebook in OneNote Online		In Navigation pane, click desired section, click desired page. On page, click in desired location below title, type web address, press spacebar or Enter.
view screenshots taken with Windows logo key + Print Screen key	Screenshots	In File Explorer, double-click *Pictures* folder, double-click *Screenshots* folder.

Recheck

Workbook

Chapter study tools, exercises, and assessments are available in the Workbook, which is accessed through your ebook.

Chapter **6**

Precheck

Customizing and Maintaining Windows

Windows 10 is very customizable. You can adjust the way input devices like a keyboard and mouse work, what colors the display uses, how loud the volume is when playing sounds and music, and much more. You can also adjust technical settings such as how the computer interacts with networks and how often it runs certain maintenance processes.

There are two main utilities for adjusting settings in Windows 10: the Control Panel and the Settings app. This chapter explains how to work with both, as well as how to adjust sound and display settings, how to connect to wireless networks, and how to make sure the computer's security, maintenance, and update settings are configured correctly.

If your computer is part of a network at school or at work, there may be IT professionals who manage your PC's settings, and your user account might be restricted from making certain system changes or using certain maintenance utilities. If you run into problems reviewing and changing system settings covered in this chapter, make sure that you have the needed permissions before assuming Windows is malfunctioning.

Skills You Learn

1 Explore the Control Panel and the Settings App

2 Personalize the Desktop

3 Modify Screen Brightness and Resolution

4 Adjust the Sound Volume

5 Connect to and Disconnect from a Wireless Network

6 Review Security, Maintenance, and Update Settings

 SNAP If you are a SNAP user, go to your SNAP Assignments page to complete the Precheck, Tutorials, and Recheck.

Files You Use

For these skills, you do not need any student data files.

Explore the Control Panel and the Settings App

The *Control Panel* and the *Settings app* are the two main areas of Windows 10 for adjusting settings and performing maintenance. Some settings appear in both places, while other settings are in only one or the other. This skill illustrates how both utilities work.

Tutorial

❶ Another Way
Click in the search box, type control panel, and then click *Control Panel Desktop app* in the search results list.

 TIP

By default, the Control Panel appears in Category view, which organizes the available settings into categories.

TIP

Large icons view allows you to browse an alphabetical list of settings, which is useful if you don't know which category the desired setting is in.

Explore the Control Panel

① Right-click the Start button and then click *Control Panel* at the shortcut menu.

② Click the *View by* box arrow and then click *Large icons* at the drop-down list.

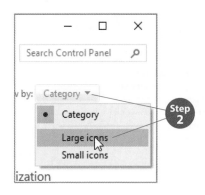

③ Click the *View by* box arrow again and then click *Category* to return to the default view.

④ Click <u>System and Security</u> to display the settings in that category.

⑤ Click <u>System</u> to display basic information about your computer.

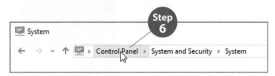

⑥ In the Address bar, click *Control Panel* to return to the top level of the Control Panel.

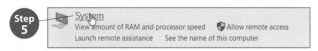

7 In the Address bar, click in the search box and then type keyboard to display a list of settings you can change for the keyboard.

8 Click <u>Change cursor blink rate</u> to open the Keyboard Properties dialog box.

9 Drag the *Cursor blink rate* slider to a moderate setting halfway between *None* and *Fast*, if it is not already set that way.

10 Click the OK button to close the Keyboard Properties dialog box.

11 Click the Close button to close the Control Panel window.

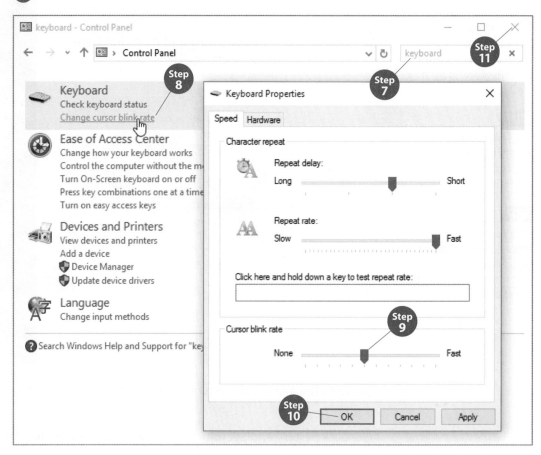

Explore the Settings App

Tutorial

12 Click the Start button.

13 Click *Settings*.

14 Click *System*.

12–13 *Another Way*
Click in the search box on the Windows taskbar, type settings, and then click *Settings Trusted Windows Store app* in the search results list.

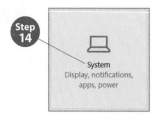

In Step 15, if you do not see the Navigation pane, widen the Settings window.

15 In the Navigation pane, click *About* to display basic information about your computer.

16 Click the Back arrow to return to the main screen of the Settings app.

TIP

In Step 15, you might need to scroll down in the Navigation pane to find *About*.

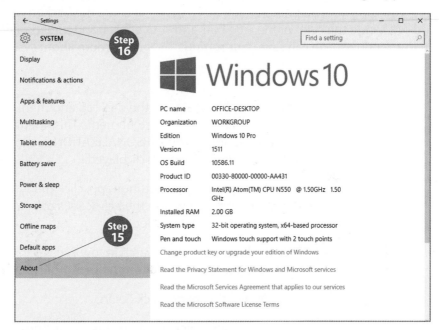

17 Click in the Settings app search box and then type mouse to display a list of mouse settings.

18 Click *Mouse & touchpad settings* in the search results list.

TIP

In the search results list, items with a cog icon represent settings you can adjust in the Settings app. Items with a different icon represent settings you can adjust in other locations.

TIP

The mouse settings you can adjust in the Settings app are basic; many more options are available in the Control Panel.

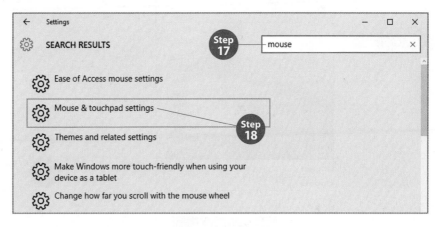

19 Examine the mouse settings available.

20 Click the Close button to close the Settings app.

Skill Extra

Responding to User Account Control (UAC) Prompts When Changing Settings

Some of the settings you can change require you to be signed in with an administrator account. This type of account is authorized to make changes that affect the entire system, not just one user's settings. In the Control Panel, such settings are identified by a small shield icon (🛡). If you are signed in with a standard (regular) account when you attempt to access such settings, you will be prompted to type the password for an administrator account.

Personalize the Desktop

You can change a variety of appearance settings to make your desktop reflect your personal preferences. For example, you can choose a photo to appear as the background or change the color of the Title bars and borders on the windows. You can save your settings as a theme and switch between themes whenever you like. A *theme* is a stored collection of settings that include the background image, window color, sound effects, and screen saver. (See the Skill Extra section to learn more about system sounds and screen savers.)

Tutorial

1 Right-click a blank area of the desktop and then click *Personalize* at the shortcut menu. This opens the Settings app to the PERSONALIZATION section with the Background page displayed.

2 In the right pane of the Settings app, click the *Background* box arrow and then click *Solid color* at the drop-down list, if needed.

3 Click the lavender color swatch in row 2, column 1 to choose it as a solid color for the background.

4 In the Navigation pane, click *Colors*.

5 In the right pane, click the *Automatically pick an accent color from my background* toggle to set it to *Off* if it is not already off.

6 In the *Choose your accent color* section, click the pink swatch in row 1, column 2.

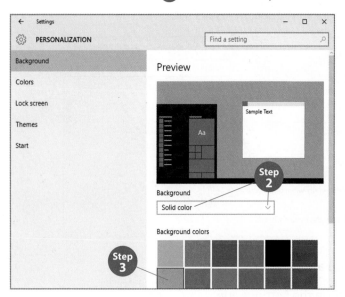

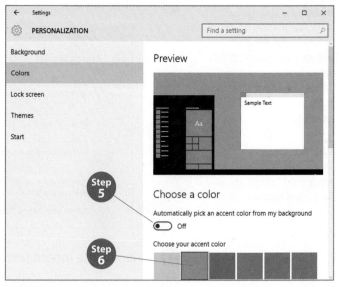

TIP

In Step 7, you may need to scroll down to see the *Show color on Start, taskbar, and action center* toggle.

7 Below the color swatches, click the *Show color on Start, taskbar, action center, and title bar* toggle to set it to *On*, if necessary. The color you chose in Step 6 is applied to the Start menu, Windows taskbar buttons, and Action Center.

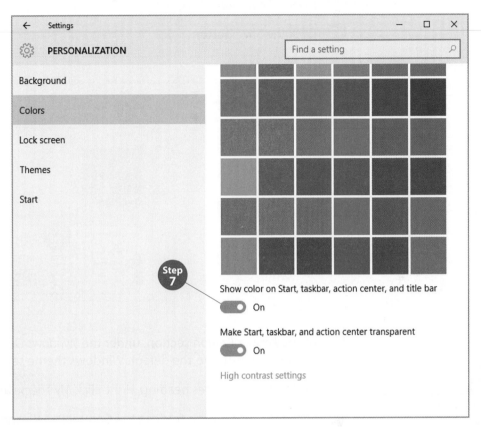

8 Click the *Show color on Start, taskbar, action center, and title bar* toggle again to set it to *Off*.

9 In the Navigation pane, click *Themes*.

10 In the right pane, click *Theme settings* to switch over to the *Personalization* section of the Control Panel.

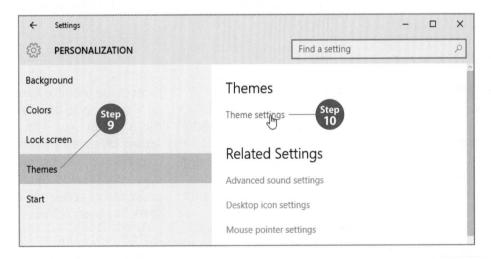

11 At the *Personalization* section, notice that the color choices you made earlier appear as an unsaved theme. Click <u>Save theme</u> to open the Save Theme As dialog box.

12 In the *Theme name* box, type My Theme.

13 Click the Save button.

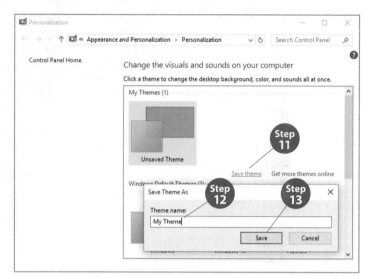

14 At the *Personalization* section, under the *Windows Default Themes* heading, click *Windows* to return to the default Windows theme settings.

TIP

If your school uses a different theme as its default, choose that in Step 15. Check with your instructor if you have questions.

15 Under the *My Themes* heading, right-click *My Theme* and then click *Delete theme*.

16 Click the Close button to close the Control Panel window.

17 Click the Close button to close the Settings app.

TIP

If you don't see *Delete theme* in Step 16, repeat Step 15. You cannot delete the active theme.

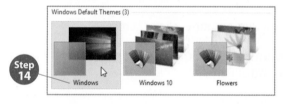
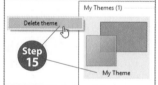

Skill Extra

Personalizing System Sounds and Screen Savers

Saving a theme also saves system sound and screen saver choices. *System sounds* are the sounds assigned to various system events, like starting up, shutting down, and displaying an error message. You can assign different sounds to various events if you don't like the default ones, or even remove all sound from a certain event if you prefer not to be notified in this way. Overall volume settings and relative volume settings are explored in Skill 4 of this chapter.

A *screen saver* is a moving image that appears onscreen after a specified period of idleness. Its original purpose is now obsolete: screen savers were designed to

protect the monitor hardware from being damaged if an image stayed onscreen for too long at a time, but this is not an issue with modern monitors. Currently, screen savers are used to obscure the screen's content to prevent others from snooping while you are away from your PC. You can set Windows to require a password to access the desktop again after the screen saver has been active.

System sound and screen saver settings are not available in the Settings app. In the Control Panel, click *Appearance and Personalization* and then, under the *Personalization* heading, click either *Change sound effects* or *Change screen saver*.

Modify Screen Brightness and Resolution

Display *brightness* is the amount of light that the screen generates. Most monitors look best at maximum brightness. However, a brighter image uses more power, so if battery life is an issue, you might choose to run at less than maximum brightness to save power. Windows can manage the brightness level automatically if you allow it to do so, dimming the display when running on battery power and brightening it again when running on AC power.

Screen resolution is the number of *pixels* (individually colored dots) vertically and horizontally that make up the display. It is usually described as two numbers, like this: 1366 x 768. The first number is the number

of pixels horizontally, and the second number is the number of pixels vertically.

The higher the resolution, the smaller text and icons will appear in Windows, and the sharper and crisper the screen will look. When Windows installs, it automatically sets itself up for the highest resolution that the display adapter and monitor support. If you run Windows in a lower resolution than the monitor's maximum, the screen image might look fuzzy. For this reason, most people prefer to run Windows in their monitor's maximum resolution. However, your instructor might ask you to set the resolution in a specific way for an individual assignment or project.

Tutorial

> **TIP**
>
> The *Brightness level* slider may not be available on your computer. If you do not see this control in Step 2, you can use brightness controls on the monitor itself.

> **TIP**
>
> In Step 3, you might need to scroll down in the dialog box to see *Advanced display settings*.

1 Right-click a blank area of the desktop and then click *Display settings* to open the Settings app to the SYSTEM section with the Display page active.

2 Drag the *Adjust brightness level* slider all the way to the right, to the brightest level (100).

3 Click *Advanced display settings*.

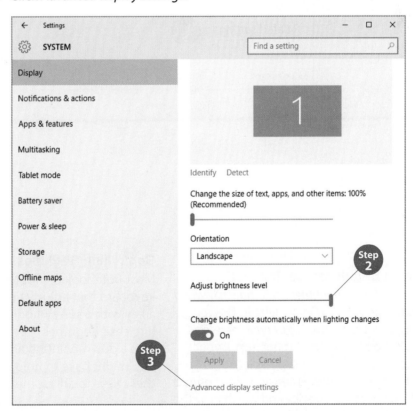

TIP

The list of available screen resolutions varies depending on the monitor.

4 Click the *Resolution* box arrow and then click a different screen resolution at the drop-down list.

5 Click the Apply button.

6 At the confirmation box, click the Keep changes button.

7 Repeat Steps 4–6 to change back to the original resolution.

8 Click the Close button to close the Settings app.

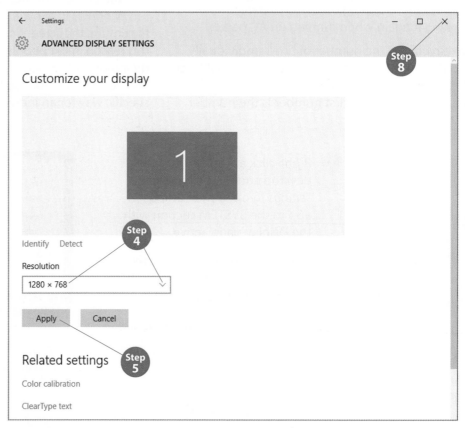

Skill Extras

Exploring the Automatic Screen Brightness Control

In Windows 10, the *Change brightness automatically when lighting changes* toggle is set to *On* by default. This toggle is located immediately below the *Adjust brightness level* slider in the *Display* section of the Settings app. If you have a portable computer (notebook or tablet), try this experiment: Make sure this setting is on and then connect or disconnect AC power to the device and watch how the screen brightness changes.

Controlling Brightness with the Keyboard

Most notebook computers have buttons on the keyboard that adjust the display brightness. Look for a key with a sun symbol plus an up-pointing arrow (Increase Brightness key) and a key with a sun symbol plus a down-pointing arrow (Decrease Brightness key). You might have to hold down the Fn key as you press these keys to adjust the brightness level.

Skill 4

Adjust the Sound Volume

Most computers have sound support, which allows you to hear sounds when system events occur like starting up and shutting down. Sound support also enables you to play music on your PC.

Windows includes a volume control in the notification area of the Windows taskbar, providing a quick shortcut for adjusting the overall volume of sounds on the PC. You can also adjust the volumes individually for different kinds of sounds. For example, you might make the volume for your music player application louder than the volume for system sounds. You can also mute the sound entirely.

Tutorial

TIP

The name of the icon you click in Step 1 might be Speakers/Headphones, depending on your computer's hardware.

1 In the notification area of the Windows taskbar, click the Speakers icon to display the volume control box.

2 Drag the slider to adjust the volume to level 56.

3 Click the Mute Speakers button to turn off all sounds.

4 Click the Unmute Speakers button to turn on all sounds.

5 Click any blank area of the desktop to close the volume control box.

Skill Extras

Adjusting the Relative Volumes of Different Applications

You can use the Sound Mixer to control the volume for an individual application or output device. In the notification area of the Windows taskbar, right-click the Speakers icon and then click *Open Volume Mixer*. Individual sliders and Mute/Unmute buttons appear for Speakers, System Sounds, and other active sound-producing applications or devices. For example, if Windows Media Player or iTunes is open, there will be a separate slider and Mute/Unmute button for it.

Adjusting the Recording Volume

If your computer has a microphone or other audio input devices, you can control their volume. In the notification area of the Windows taskbar, right-click the Speakers icon and then click *Recording devices* to open the Sound dialog box with the Recording tab active. Double-click the desired recording device (for example, *Microphone*) to open its Properties box and then set its volume on the Levels tab. Click OK twice to close the open dialog boxes when finished.

Troubleshooting Sound Problems

If the sound isn't playing as expected on your computer, right-click the Speakers icon in the notification area of the Windows taskbar and then click *Troubleshoot sound problems*. Follow the prompts in the Playing Audio troubleshooter that appears.

Connect to and Disconnect from a Wireless Network

If you use a computer that has wireless networking capability, you might use it to connect to a Wi-Fi hotspot. A *hotspot* is a wireless router, a connection box that can communicate with wireless-enabled devices via radio frequency (RF) waves. *Wi-Fi* is the informal nickname for the standard that almost all hotspots use; its technical name is *IEEE 802.11*. Most Wi-Fi hotspots have a range of about 100 feet.

If your computer is already connected to a wireless network, the Wireless icon appears in the notification area of the Windows taskbar, like this: . Your PC's network adapter can be connected to only one wireless network at a time, so when you connect to a different network, you automatically disconnect from the previous one.

When wireless networks are available but your computer is not currently connected to any of them,

the Wireless icon appears in the notification area with a small star in its upper left corner, like this: . You can choose to have your computer connect to a particular Wi-Fi hotspot whenever it is within range, so you don't have to go through the connection process every time you want to connect.

A *secure router* is one that has some sort of password protection on it. A *security key* is like a password for the router. Security keys are the standard way of connecting to a secure router. If you are connecting to a secure router in your workplace, at school, or in a public place, you will probably use a security key. A *PIN* (personal identification number) is an alternative to a security key, and is an option mainly on small routers sold for personal home use.

Note: *You will need a computer with wireless capability and access to a wireless network to complete this skill.*

Tutorial

TIP

The networks you see will be different from the ones shown in this skill.

TIP

In Step 2, if only one network is listed and you are already connected to it, click it, click the Disconnect button, and then click the network again to select it.

1 In the notification area of the Windows taskbar, click the Wireless icon to display a pane listing the available networks.

2 Click the desired network (*Sycamore_Knoll* in the example shown).

3 **Optional:** Click the *Connect automatically* check box to insert a check mark if you want your PC to connect to this network automatically in the future.

4 Click the Connect button.

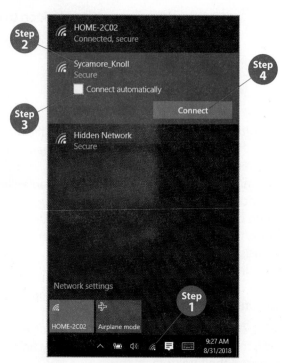

5 If prompted to enter a PIN or security key, complete the appropriate step below. **Note:** *Check with your instructor if you need help.*

5a *Another Way*
Routers that support PINs also support security keys. When prompted to enter a PIN, if you prefer, you can click Connect using a security key instead and follow the instructions in Step 5b.

5a To connect using a PIN: Type the 8-digit PIN printed on your router's label and then click the Next button.

5b To connect using a security key: Type the network security key and then click the Next button.

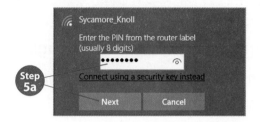

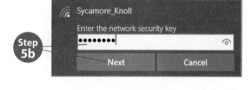

6 If this is the first time you have connected to this network, a prompt appears asking if you want to find content automatically on the network. Choose one of two options:

6a If this is a home or work network, click Yes to turn on file sharing so you can exchange files with other users.

6b If this is a school or public network, click No to disable file sharing so others will not be able to browse your files.

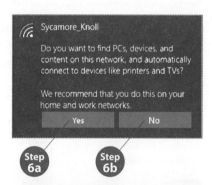

7 Click outside the wireless pane to close it.

8 In the notification area of the Windows taskbar, click the Wireless icon.

9 Click the network that shows *Connected* under its name.

10 Click the Disconnect button.

11 Click outside the wireless pane to close it.

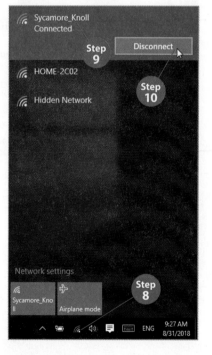

Skill Extra

Using Airplane Mode

Airplane mode temporarily disables your Wi-Fi hardware so that it doesn't search for or connect to a wireless network. To use it, click the Wireless icon in the notification area of the Windows taskbar and then click *Airplane mode*. To return to regular functionality, click the Wireless icon again and then click *Wi-Fi*. Airplane mode, as the name implies, is useful when you are using your computer in an environment where Wi-Fi usage is not permitted, such as on an airplane during a flight.

Skill 6

Review Security, Maintenance, and Update Settings

Windows 10 is mostly self-maintaining. The correct settings are enabled automatically to ensure trouble-free operation for most users. The *Security and Maintenance* section of the Control Panel summarizes the status of important security and maintenance areas and lets you know if any action is recommended. The *Windows Update* section of the Settings app allows you to check for Windows updates.

Tutorial

TIP

You may need special permission to open some of the security features described in this skill.

TIP

Messages with a red bar are important problems to be addressed. Messages with a yellow bar are warnings and might not need action.

TIP

The messages you see in Steps 3–5 may be different from the ones shown here.

Review Security and Maintenance Settings

1. Right-click the Start button and then click *Control Panel*.

2. Under the *System and Security* heading, click <u>Review your computer's status</u>.

> **Step 2**
>
> System and Security
> Review your computer's status
> Save backup copies of your files with File History
> Backup and Restore (Windows 7)
> Find and fix problems

3. Under the *Security* heading, review any messages with a red or yellow bar and take the appropriate action. ***Note:*** *Ask your instructor if you are unsure what to do about a message.*

4. Click the down-pointing *Security* heading arrow to display more security settings.

5. Scroll though the list of security settings to review their status.

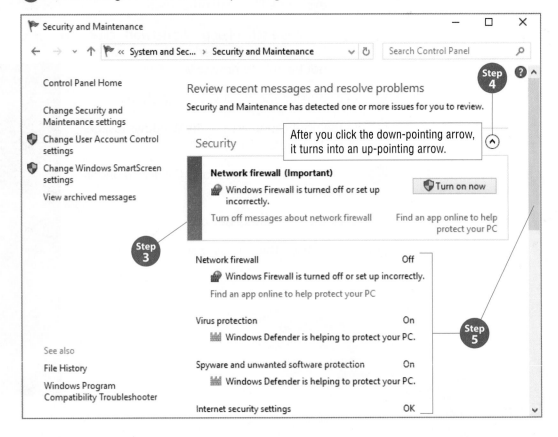

6 Click the up-pointing *Security* heading arrow to collapse the section.

7 Click the down-pointing *Maintenance* heading arrow to review maintenance settings.

8 Scroll through the list of maintenance settings to review their status. For example, note the last run date in the *Automatic Maintenance* section.

9 Click the Close button to close the window.

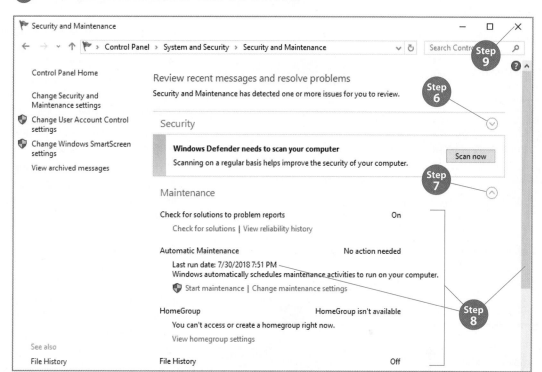

TIP

Settings that have a Change settings link can be modified by clicking that option. If there is a shield symbol next to the option, making changes requires administrator permission.

TIP

In Step 11, you might need to scroll down to see the Update & security button.

TIP

In Step 13, you can close the Settings app while the updates are being downloaded and installed; the process will continue. The Settings app might close automatically.

10 Click the Start button and then click Settings.

11 Click *Update & security* to open the *Windows Update* section.

12 Click the Check for updates button if it appears, and wait for the check to complete. If any updates are found, they are downloaded and installed automatically. You might see a notice that a restart has been scheduled for installing updates.

13 Click the Close button to close the Settings app.

Skill Extra

Controlling Automatic Update Installation

In the Settings app's *Windows Update* section, you can click *Advanced options* to display a screen that contains a *Choose how updates are installed* drop-down list. The default is *Automatic (recommended)*. If you prefer, you can choose *Notify to schedule restart*. This option delays any updates that require a restart until you give your permission for the restart to happen.

Task Summary

Task	Button/Icon/Option	Action
adjust sound volume	Speakers (High Definition Audio Device) ◁) 56	In Windows taskbar notification area, click Speakers icon, drag slider, click away to close slider.
apply default theme	Windows	In *Personalization* section of Control Panel, under *Windows Default Themes* heading, click *Windows*.
change desktop colors	Background	In Navigation pane of *Personalization* section of Settings app, click *Background*, click *Background* drop-down list box arrow, click *Solid color*, click color swatch. In Navigation pane, click *Colors*, set *Automatically pick an accent color from my background* toggle to *Off*, click color swatch, set *Show color on Start, taskbar, and action center* to On.
change screen brightness (laptop)	Brightness level	At desktop, right-click any blank area, click *Display settings*, drag *Brightness level* slider.
change screen resolution	Resolution 1280 × 768	At desktop, right-click any blank area, click *Display settings*, click *Advanced display settings*, click *Resolution* drop-down list box arrow, click desired resolution, click Apply, click Keep Changes.
check for Windows Updates	Update & security Windows Update, recovery, backup	Click Start button, click *Settings*. At Settings app, click *Update & security*, click Check for updates button.
connect to a wireless network	*⁄⁄	In Windows taskbar notification area, click Wireless icon, click desired network, click Connect button, type PIN or security key and click Next if prompted to do so.
delete theme	Delete theme	In *Personalization* section of Control Panel, under *My Themes*, right-click theme, click *Delete theme*.
disconnect from a wireless network	⁄⁄	In Windows taskbar notification area, click Wireless icon, click connected network, click Disconnect button, click outside pane to close it.
mute/unmute sound	◁)) ◁×	In Windows taskbar notification area, click Speakers icon, click Mute Speakers/Unmute Speakers.
open Control Panel	Control Panel	Right-click Start button, click *Control Panel*.
open *Personalization* section of Settings app	Personalize	At desktop, right-click any blank area, click *Personalize*.
open Settings app	⚙ Settings	Click Start button, click *Settings*.
review security and maintenance settings	System and Security Review your computer's status	Right-click Start button, click *Control Panel*. Under *System and Security*, click Review your computer's status.
save new theme after changing desktop colors	Themes	After changing desktop colors and before closing Settings app, click *Themes* in Navigation pane, click *Theme settings*. In Control Panel, click Save theme. In Save Theme As dialog box, type name in *Theme name* box, click Save.

Recheck   Workbook

Chapter study tools, exercises, and assessments are available in the Workbook, which is accessed through your ebook.

Glossary and Index

Cortana Microsoft's user-friendly search tool, capable of responding to English language requests either via voice or typing. 34
  searching files for using, 36
  searching Web using, 36
  using to get information online, 48
  Windows taskbar access, 3
customizing
  Account button, 54
  options for, 4

D

data file A file that stores data a user has entered using a computer, such as a word processing document. 29
deleting
  browser history, 45–46
  files, 32–33
  files and folders in OneDrive, 56
  files using keyboard commands, 32
  turning off confirmations, 33
desktop application A type of application designed to run on the Windows desktop; prior to Windows 8, this was the only type of application available. *See also* **Modern app,** 6
  examples, 6
desktop The background area of the Windows interface. *See also* **desktop application,** 3
  personalizing, 80–82
  working with multiple, 10
dialog box A window that prompts the user to provide additional information about a command or action being taken. 11
  using, 12
Disk Cleanup utility, 32
display brightness. *See* **brightness,** 83
Dogpile, 42
download To transfer a file from the Internet to your computer. *See also* **upload,** 57
  executable files, 25
  files from website, 43

keyboard command, 40
reducing malware risk, 43
ZIP files, 24–25
drag-and-drop To move or copy an onscreen item to a different location by pointing to it, holding down the left mouse button, and moving the mouse. 29
  files or folders onto icon, 31
  moving and copying files using, 29–30
dragging and pointing, 4
drop-down lists, 12, 13

E

editing
  Reading view and, 60
  read-only access and, 61
email
  changing or setting default application, 68
  confirmation of sending, 68
  images using Snipping Tool, 68
  sharing OneNote content via, 74
Error icon, 58
Esc key, 4
executable files, downloading, 25
extension A code that appears following a file name to indicate the file's type, such as .txt or .docx. 16
external drives and Recycle Bin, 32, 33

F

favorite A saved URL in a web browser. 44
  saving and reopening, 44
Favorites Bar, saving to, 44
Favorites list A list of saved URLs in a web browser. 44
file A collection of computer instructions or data saved with a name, such as myfile.txt. 16
  copying and pasting a group of files, 16
  copying and pasting in OneDrive, 56
  copying and pasting using copy and paste, 30–31

copying and pasting using drag-and-drop, 29–30
copying and pasting using keyboard commands, 31
copying and pasting using Move To button on Home tab, 31
deleting, 32–33
deleting in OneDrive, 56
downloading from website, 43
editing in online application, 60
hiding, 19–20
meaning of extensions, 16
OneDrive, 55
renaming, 22
renaming guidelines, 22
renaming in OneDrive, 56
retrieving deleted, 16
searching for using Cortana, 36
searching for using File Explorer Search Box, 34–35
searching inside, 34
selecting in OneDrive, 56
selecting location, 59
selecting multiple, 26
showing hidden, 19–20
uploading to OneDrive, 57–58
File Explorer
  clicking to open item, 55
  closing, 8
  as default pinned button, 3
  navigating between local volumes and folders, 17–18
  panes, 17
  ribbon visibility, 20, 21
  searching for files using Search Box, 34–35
  showing file extension, 20–21
  using, 16
  using, to access OneDrive, 51–52
File Explorer button, 7
file extension. *See* **extension**
file list pane, on File Explorer, 17
Firefox, viewing and clearing browser history, 46
folder A computer version of a paper folder, serving as an organizational unit to manage groups of files. 16

choosing which, to sync, 52

copying and pasting in OneDrive, 56

creating, 22–23

default OneDrive, 55

deleting in OneDrive, 56

pinned shortcuts to, 17

renaming, 22

renaming guidelines, 22

renaming in OneDrive, 56

selecting in OneDrive, 56

selecting multiple, 26

sharing, from OneDrive, 61

Free-from Snip, 66

Full-screen Snip, 66

G

Goodsearch, 42

Google Chrome, viewing and clearing browser history, 46

graphics. *See also* **screenshot**

file formats available, 64

H

hamburger button, 5

hard disk contents, 29

help. *See also* **Cortana**

getting, 14

troubleshooting sound problems, 85

troubleshooting wireless network problems, 14

hidden files, showing, 19–20

history. *See* **browser history,** 45

hotspot A wireless router that makes network or Internet access available. Many hotspots are public, meaning anyone may use them. 86

typical range, 86

Hub button, 44

hyperlink

address, 61

emailing, to OneNote content, 74

inserting in OneNote page, 72–73

I

icon A small picture onscreen representing a file or program. 3

advantage of large, 77

changing size, 18

cog, in Settings app, 79

dragging, 4

dragging-and-dropping files or folders on, 31

shield, 79

Wireless, 86

IEEE 802.11 The standard governing Wi-Fi, the most popular wireless networking technology. IEEE stands for Institute of Electrical and Electronics Engineers. 86

images. *See also* **screenshot**

file formats available, 64

inserting in OneNote page, 72

using Snipping Tool to email, 68

interfaces, types, 11

Internet Explorer

automatic default from Microsoft Edge, 39

viewing and clearing browser history, 46

item check boxes, displaying, 21

K

keyboard commands

closing File Explorer window, 8

closing windows, 10

copying and pasting web address in OneNote, 73

copying files, 31

deleting files, 32

downloading, 40

moving and resizing windows, 8

pasting, 65

printing, 64

screen brightness, 84

selecting multiple files and folders, 26

L

landscape orientation, 47

link

address, 61

emailing, to OneNote content, 74

inserting in OneNote page, 72–73

lists, expanded, 17

Lock screen, 2

M

maintenance settings, reviewing, 88–89

malware Software that causes annoying or harmful effects when run. 43

reducing download risk, 43

maximize To enlarge a window to fill the entire screen. 7

window automatically by snapping app, 8

Maximize button, 7

menu, closing, 4

menu button, 5

menu system A control system in some applications in which you click a word on a menu bar across the top of the window to open a drop-down menu of commands. 11

apps using, 11

using, 11–12

messages with red bar, meaning of, 88

Microsoft Edge Microsoft's web browser software, new in Windows 10. 38

as default browser, 39

as default pinned button, 3

Internet Explorer and, 39

tabbed browsing, 40

Microsoft Office Online

creating new document using, 59

editing files in, 60

free, simplified versions, 50

saving edits, 60

Microsoft OneNote Microsoft's application for collecting and organizing information from multiple locations and in multiple formats. 63

adding content to page in, 70–71

creating notebook, sections, and pages in, 69

printing online notebook page, 71

sharing content via email, 74

using Clipboard with, 72–73

minimize To shrink a window so that it appears only as a button

renaming
  files and folders, 22
  files and folders in OneDrive, 56
resizing. *See also* **maximize; minimize; restore**
  icon, 18
  web pages, 42
  windows, 7–8
Restore Down button, 7
restore To change a window's size so that it is neither minimized nor maximized. 7
ribbon A type of toolbar used in many applications in which multiple tabbed pages of commands are available. 11
  apps using, 11
  Move To button on Home tab, 31
  using, 12–13
  using contextual tabs on, 13
  visibility in File Explorer, 20, 21

S

saving
  favorites, 44
  Favorites Bar to, 44
screen brightness. *See* **brightness**
screen capture. *See* **screenshot**, 63
screen resolution The number of pixels horizontally and vertically comprising a display, such as 1366 x 768. The first number is the width; the second the height. 83
  monitor and available, 84
  understanding, 83
screen saver A utility that blanks the screen or shows a moving pattern on it after a specified period of user inactivity. 82
  personalizing, 82
screenshot A digital image of the contents of your display screen at a given moment. 63
  annotating snips captured, 66–67
  capturing, of entire screen, 64–65
  saving in different file format, 64
  using snipping tool to capture part of, 66–67
search box The box on the

Windows taskbar to the right of the Start button, into which you can type keywords to search. 3
  opening and closing applications using, 6
search engine A website dedicated to indexing Internet content and making a searchable database of that information available to the public. 41
  examples, 43
  using, 41–42
section A group of related pages in a OneNote notebook. 69
  creating, 69
secure router A router that requires connecting computers to supply a security key. 86
security key A string of letters and numbers that serves as a password for a secure router. 86
security settings, reviewing, 88–89
selecting
  files and folders in OneDrive, 56
  location of files and folders, 59
  multiple files and folders, 26
  multiple files and folders using keyboard commands, 26
Settings app A Modern app in Windows 10 that provides access to a variety of user-adjustable settings. 77
  adjusting settings in, 79
  cog icon, 79
  exploring, 78–79
Settings window, customizing options, 4
shield icon, 79
shortcut An icon that is a pointer to an actual file, but is not the file itself. 3
  default pinned, 3
  multiple computer users', 17
  pinned to folders, 17
shut down To quit Windows and power down the computer. 2
sign in To identify yourself by entering your credentials (user name and password) in Windows and other applications. 2

OneDrive, 53–54
  Windows, step-by-step, 2
sign out To end your Windows session without shutting down the computer. 2
  methods, 2
  OneDrive, 54
SIT archive files, 28
Sleep, 2
Snipping Tool An application that enables users to capture a screenshot of a part of the computer screen. 66
  types of snips, 66
  using, to email image, 68
  using to capture part of screen, 66–67
sound
  adjusting volume, 85
  troubleshooting problems, 85
Sound Mixer, 85
speaker icon, 4
Start button The button in the lower left corner of the Windows desktop; when clicked it opens the Start menu. 3
Start menu A menu of commands and applications a user can access to run programs, manage files, and perform other activities in Windows. 3
  opening, 3
  shortcut tiles pinned to, 5
support, getting, 14
sync Short for synchronize; generally refers to updating copies of data files stored in multiple locations so that all copies are the same. 51
  choosing which folders to, 52
system sounds Sounds that play when certain system events happen in the operating system, such as starting up, shutting down, or an error occurring. 82
  personalizing, 82

T

tabbed browsing, using, 40
TAR archive files, 28